STRICTLY STEAK

D1125086

LI

STRICTLY STEAK

*A Passionate Guide to the
Great American Feast*

A. D. Livingston

BURFORD BOOKS

Printed in the United States of America

10 9 8 7 6 5 4 3 2 1

Library of Congress Cataloging-in-Publication Data
Livingston, A. D., 1932–
    Strictly steak / by A. D. Livingston.
       p.   cm.
    Includes index.
    ISBN 1-58080-048-3 (pbk).
    1. Cookery (Beef).   I. Title.
TX749.5.B43 L58   2000
641.6'62—dc21   99-059657

Other Cookbooks by A. D. Livingston

Cast-Iron Cooking

On the Grill

Sausage

Cold-Smoking and Salt-Curing Meats, Fish, and Game

Venison Cookbook

Complete Fish & Game Cookbook

Contents

ACKNOWLEDGMENTS

THE AUTHOR WOULD like to thank the friends, guests, and cooks who have contributed to this book. Specific acknowledgments to individuals, other books, and authors are made in the text as appropriate. A few of the recipes and a little of the text were used, in slightly altered form, in the author's column for *Gray's Sporting Journal*.

INTRODUCTION

~~~~~~~~~~~~~~~~~

SOMETHING CULINARILY SUBVERSIVE is afoot here in America. Slowly, insidiously, surely, red meat is being squeezed out of the American diet, a response to nutritional fanatics who live in constant fear of common table salt and good red meat. In some cookbooks, for example, we find instructions on how to carve a T-bone or porterhouse steak so that it can be served equitably to several people, and in slick magazines we see pretty photographs of a little dab of meat surrounded by a few sprigs of green stuff, artfully arranged. As the meat portion dwindles, we are being fed all manner of stuff with our steaks, including such fill-ups as pasta and dried beans.

Now don't misunderstand me. I love pasta and consider it necessary for a spaghetti dinner. I truly love good Boston baked beans served with barbecued pork ribs. I even like spinach, but I was quite surprised to read on the dust jacket of one modern and somewhat prissified book that creamed spinach is the classic accompaniment for steaks. Classic? Not in Kansas City. Somehow, to my taste and to my mind's eye, the juices of spinach and steak just don't make an appetizing mix. Maybe that's part of the plot.

In this book, we won't serve up beans and pasta and spinach with little pieces of meat, carefully carved and measured. Everybody gets a big T-bone on his plate, leaving only enough room for a baked potato on one side and perhaps a few spears of steamed asparagus on the other. Bread and salad are served separately. This simplifies the cooking, the menu, and the serving. It also affords the cook the big culinary advantage of sending the steak straight to the table, sizzling hot off the grill, instead of having to keep it warm while the guests linger on and on with several preliminary courses. I might also add that a steak has no place on the table with the typical Thanksgiving turkey, dressing, baked ham, and so on. It just doesn't fit. Nor is steak an everyday feast for most of us, often for financial reasons and sometimes for legitimate health's sake. There is probably a limit to how much red meat we should eat. But from time to time nothing beats a big gustatory steak dinner, which is really easy to prepare and quick to fix—an important consideration in some modern homes in which both the man and the woman work.

In keeping with this spirit, I have focused the recipes in this book on the steak itself, something to be enjoyed for its own sake. I have, however, added a chapter on go-withs and another on sauces, sops, and rubs. Most of the recipes in the main are for beefsteaks, but I do have few comments and suggestions on cooking steaks from pork, venison, mutton, and so on. These are sometimes called chops, but the shape and thickness and methods of cooking qualify them as steaks, I say. I have also included a steak or two cut from large birds such as ostrich and turkey, along with a note on fish and alligator steaks.

So, what *is* a steak? It's simply a slab of meat from 1 to 2 inches thick, as large as your hand or, preferably, larger. A steak is cut across the grain, whereas a fillet goes with the grain, with a few exceptions. The various cuts of beefsteaks are discussed in a chapter over toward the end of the book, followed with a shorter chapter on other steaks and chops.

My instinct was to start this book off by cooking steak in the first chapter without the usual background material and tedious introductory chapters. After all, everybody knows what a T-bone is. So, let's finish a few odds and ends here before cooking steaks. We can be eating in 30 minutes.

Tools and Steakmanship

Many cooks say they can tell when a steak is done by the touch method. I have a problem with this, and, personally, I don't want some good ol' boy poking his finger into my steak all during the grilling. Experience and a good eye help the cook to tell when a steak is done, and a timer and meat thermometer are great teaching aids. The ultimate test, however, is to slice into a steak at the thickest part. (The chef should cut into his own steak, not that of his guests, or perhaps cook a separate steak for testing; if it is done or almost done, not too much of the good juice will run out.) If it runs blood, it's rare. If it's nicely pink and juicy inside, it's medium rare. Any cooking beyond that point is a culinary mistake. People who insist on good steaks being well done have that right and will not be turned away from my table, but I really don't enjoy cooking for them or eating with them. If the cook enjoys the job, it usually shows; if he doesn't, well, that shows, too.

In any case, I would like to discuss a few cooking tools and helpful gadgets.

TIMERS. Cooking a steak close to the heat source for a short period of time doesn't permit much margin for error. The best bet is to use a good timer. My favorite kind is fitted with a strap and is worn around the neck. That way, it sounds off and alerts me even if I have to leave the grill to get another beer or something. I usually set the timer for 3 minutes (if the steak is to be cooked for 7 or 8 minutes), which gives me a minute or so on either side for fine-tuning.

But it's a mistake to rely solely on the timer. A good slicing knife and the eye have the final say.

THERMOMETERS. Meat thermometers can be the cook's best friend when baking a roast or other large chunk of meat, but they have limited use in steak cookery. Oven thermometers and closed-hood grill thermometers check on the thermostat settings, letting the cook make adjustments up or down as needed. Also, internal meat thermometers help in cooking large chunks of meat, such as rib roasts and whole turkeys. For thick steaks, a quick-reading probe thermometer, which works somehow with a digital readout instead of a rising column of mercury, can give a quick check on what's going on inside, and these are become increasingly popular. But one should use such a probe very sparingly, because it punches holes in the steak, letting out the good juices.

MEAT-TURNING FORKS. I have no use for these and very seldom use them. They stick holes in the meat.

TONGS. These are my favorite tools for turning steaks. I insist on short spring-loaded tongs made with thin stainless steel, scalloped edges on the business ends. Those tongs with claws or toes tend to stick into the meat, and long tongs are harder to use. Most of the so-called barbecue tools on the market are simply too long for comfort and sure grip.

SPATULAS. I like a thin spring-steel spatula for turning hamburger steaks. Some cheap spatulas on the market are made of metal that is too thick, making them difficult to get under the burger without tearing it. I want a relatively short spatula. Often a second spatula is needed to help turn a hamburger steak, using one on top and one on bottom. The second spatula should be the first one's twin, so that if you can't find the one you can use the other.

Some persnickety cooks insist on turning such steaks as ribeyes with spatulas instead of tongs or forks, claiming that both tongs and forks make holes in the steak.

POTHOLDERS AND COOKING GLOVES. Good potholders are needed for handling broiler racks and skillets. The handles of cast-iron skillets get very hot, I might caution. Never use a wet potholder or wet towel; these can quickly steam up, and can burn you badly. Some potholders are square and others are designed as mittens. Either type will do. My favorite, however, is a pair of good heavy-duty leather or cooking gloves. Usually, the leather covers only the palms and the fingers, with the top being canvas or some such material. I consider these gloves to be indispensable for cooking over an open wood-coal fire.

MEAT MALLETS. These come in handy for beating a tough steak, but I often use the edge of a heavy plate or saucer. Also, the mouth of a glass bottle does a very good job. I might add that having a heavy wooden butcher block under the steak makes the beating more effective or at least more enjoyable, somehow.

PEPPER AND SALT MILLS. Pepper mills and salt mills (used for grinding coarse sea salt) should be part of a table setting. Always provide these for your guests instead of little salt and pepper shakers. The larger mills usually work best, or at least faster.

STEAK KNIVES. Many commercial steak knifes look pretty but don't work as well as they should, especially on flank steak and such cuts. Some of these have long, flimsy blades, and some have blades that are rather dull with serrated edges. The best steak knives may not be pretty. They have a short, stout blade with a large, easy-grip wooden handle. In all knives, except silverware, I prefer a carbon-steel blade. These will tarnish, but they sure do cut good if they are properly sharpened. But, alas, they are hard to find these days.

KNIFE SHARPENERS. Chefs who swish a long knife and steel together are mostly putting on a show. It's true that a steel, and some of the modern V-shaped gadgets, will align the edge of a blade, making it seem sharper. But sooner or later you'll have to remove some metal with a file or some sort of grinder. Carboloy will do, but I really prefer to use a large natural Arkansas whetstone, which is a natural rock that is quarried in Arkansas and which is getting in short supply, making it expensive, especially in the large sizes. Often many-hued like marble, these whetstones are really things of beauty and a joy to use. They've got true grit.

STEAKS ON THE GRILL

1

GRILLING MEAT OVER wood coals doesn't merely satisfy some atavistic urge to cook outside the cave. There's more to it than that. It's a hands-on kind of cooking, bringing into play the smells of wood smoke and cooking meat, the sizzle on the turn, the color of the meat. The eating is excellent, too, if the cook does his job, and a perfectly grilled porterhouse, thick and juicy, is a gustatory joy indeed.

There are, it's true, thousands of recipes for grilled steaks. But the method and technique are much more important than marinades and bastes. Attention to small detail means more—much more—than a long ingredients list. A little salt and freshly ground black pepper are all you need to grill wonderful steaks. Add anything else at your culinary peril. (Well, maybe that statement is a little too strong. Let's just say that too many herbs and spices, or too much balsamic vinegar, can be culinary distractions, if you like the flavor of beef.)

I should add here that I consider grilled steaks to be cooked on a grid of some sort directly over the heat source. Hardwood coals make the ideal heat, and, being products of an open fire, they best fulfill the mystique of the grill. Although I appreciate the practicality and convenience of using charcoal, gas heat, or electric heating elements, I see these not as advances in technology (which they are) but as setbacks from a purely culinary standpoint. Necessary, at times, and almost always more convenient than a wood fire—but nevertheless a step away from the real thing.

Other opinions are strongly held. Some people maintain that lava rocks heated by bottled propane gas and surrounded by water-soaked mesquite purchased from the store cook the best steaks. Others champion briquettes, pressed and glued to shape. Purists insist on real charcoal of irregular shape. Even hard coal has been championed. And, yes, all these methods can produce excellent steaks. So, use what you have.

I'm not going to write a text here on how to build a fire, but I personally try to avoid chemical starters, especially the squirt-bottle type. But I would be lying if I said I never used them. For convenience in starting, the electric or gas-heated grills are hard to beat.

Anyhow, here is my take on fuels, listed by order of my personal preference, with a note tacked on at the end about wood chips for smoking.

HARDWOOD FIRES. "Hardwood coals" might be a more accurate heading, but the term is too easily confused with "charcoal," and I want no mistake here. The best steaks I have ever eaten were quickly cooked over very hot coals. In spite of hotly defended regional and individual preferences, it really doesn't make much difference which kind of wood is used, provided that it is hardwood such as oak or hickory or apple. Some woods do burn hotter than others, but the technique here is much more important than subtle differences. I do, however, prefer green freshly cut hardwood to dry wood. It's true that dry wood is easier to start and burns better, but green wood makes a hotter coal and much more smoke.

Because hardwood coal gets so hot, it is important to have a heavy-duty cast-iron grate on which to cook. This grate might be fitted to a cast-iron fire box, as in the small Hibachi grills, or it might be simply placed over hot coals on the ground or in a fireplace. The fire can be built inside some large, heavy-duty grill boxes, but thin ones will quickly burn out.

I have a clever outdoor cooking tool called Big Food, which can be raised or lowered easily and which can be swung out and away from the fire. There are several other such grills available in patio grilling shops and outdoor cooking catalogs. Or you can rig your own simply by putting a grate over four bricks stood on end. Build a hardwood fire away from the cooking area, then shovel hot coals between the bricks and put the grate in place. It's best to position the steaks about 4 inches above the hot coals, but a rig that is adjustable in height is ideal. Thin steaks go close to the heat; larger steaks, farther away.

Grilling over wood coals can be a little tricky because of the intense heat. They really do get hotter than briquettes. So, watch what you are doing, especially if you are drinking beer and talking while grilling the steaks. If you don't, you'll likely burn or overcook your steaks. I recommend using a buzzer timer with a neck strap. Set it for 3 minutes per side, then make adjustments as needed. Of course, much depends on the exact setup, heat, and thickness of the steak. But a timer will keep you in the ballpark and can save the day.

See also the chapter on campfire cooking. In it I've described a raised platform to hold wood coals, which minimizes a lot of squatting.

CHARCOAL. Real charcoal is irregular in shape and has not been compressed in a mold. Its fire is not as hot as wood coals, but it's a good deal hotter than briquettes. I like charcoal very much, but it's not as easy to find as briquettes. Try retail stores that traffic in grills and patio cookery.

CHARCOAL BRIQUETTES. These are made of powdered and compressed charcoal, held together with a binder or glue of some sort. Sometimes briquettes contain quick-start additives. Although they stack neatly, the fire from briquettes simply doesn't get as hot as wood coals or real charcoal. Availability is their big advantage. You can buy 'em these days in supermarkets, convenience stores, department stores—even drugstores.

ELECTRIC HEAT. I like to cook over electric heat from time to time, and I am especially fond of the modern stoves with built-in grills, featuring a powerful down-draft fan that pulls the smoke out of the house. In my experience, however, most of the electric units, indoor or out, don't produce quite enough heat for direct grilling. They will work, sure, but not quite perfectly.

GAS HEAT. I am aware of the popularity of these units. They will do a good job, especially when used with plenty of lava rocks. They will get hot enough, in most cases, and are very easy to light. I don't, however, like to cook directly over gas fumes. Some people tell me this is in my head, but, nonetheless, I don't like the idea. Yet, I'll have to allow that I've eaten some very good steaks cooked over gas.

The best gas grills are large and have a hood, making indirect cooking easy. These are fueled by relatively large propane tanks. It's always best to have two tanks—one full standby tank, and one in use.

For some of us who tend to procrastinate, maintenance can be a problem with gas grills, and the burner elements are often in need of replacement. If some of the small holes in the burner elements clog with grease and others burn out (making large holes), your beautiful sirloin might turn out rare on one end and burnt on the other, or with holes in the middle.

HARD COAL. This excellent fuel is hard to find these days in most areas. It does, however, make a very hot fire, and the coals burn for a long time. If hard coal were more readily available in reasonably small quantities, I would move it up higher on this list of grilling fuels.

WOOD CHIPS. These are added to the heat to produce smoke. They are not a primary source of heat, and are, in fact, often soaked in water to prevent them from burning up. The best chips are from freshly cut green wood, and don't have to be soaked. The size of the chips varies, and some are billed as "chunks." Even wood sawdust is used to produce smoke. All these are good for indirect cooking and smoking, but don't work as well for direct grilling, partly because the cooking time is quite short. Also, in my opinion, smoke, like tomato-based barbecue sauces, doesn't really enhance the flavor of beef very much and goes better with pork. I'll get some arguments on that one.

In any case, most of the recipes below can be cooked success-fully with any of the various heats and with almost any grill. The only requirement is that the metal rack be close to the heat source, allow-ing quick cooking, and it should be adjustable to cook thick or thin steaks. In most of the recipes I recommend that the steaks be grilled uncovered. Exceptions are noted in the individual recipes.

A. D.'S WOOD-FIRE STEAK

Build a good hardwood fire. While waiting for the fire to burn down to hot coals, brush the steaks lightly on each side with a mixture of Myron's 20-Gauge wild game sauce (see chapter 12) and a little olive oil. Stack the steaks one atop the other and leave them out, letting them reach room temperature. When you have plenty of coals, rake some away from the main fire. Position a cast-iron grill (or rack) about 3 inches over the coals. Using tongs, lay the steaks on the grill. Cook for 3 minutes. Turn and cook for 2 or 3 minutes. Turn, sprin-kle with salt (lightly) and pepper, and add a pat or two of butter. Cook until the steaks are medium rare. Serve hot.

COWBELLES' T-BONES FOR TWO

I adapted this recipe from *Beef Cookbook,* published by the Alabama CowBelles and Alabama Cattlemen's Association a few years back.

Mrs. E. H. Wilson of Montgomery, past president of the CowBelles, said that the recipe yields a meal "that pleases the man in your life— and didn't he have fun cooking the steak!" That's the spirit!

2 T-bones*	2 tablespoons butter
2 tablespoons Worcestershire sauce	salt and pepper

Rig for grilling. Melt the butter and stir in the Worcestershire, salt, and pepper. Brush the mixture over the steaks, front and back. Grill over hot coals for a few minutes on each side, until the steaks are rare or medium rare. Serve the steaks on a heated plate, along with a baked potato and a sprig of parsley. Serve also a large salad bowl, overflowing with lettuce, tomatoes, and other fresh vegetables and fruits. End the meal with a small piece of cherry pie and a cup of coffee, Mrs. Wilson says.

EASY TENDERLOINS

Here's an excellent way to cook small tenderloins on the grill. If you've got snooty company, call 'em filet mignon.

beef tenderloins, cut 1½ inches thick	salt and freshly ground black pepper
thin-sliced bacon	

Rig for grilling over charcoal, placing the rack about 4 inches over the heat. Sprinkle the tenderloins with salt and pepper. Wrap each one with a strip of bacon, cutting the bacon to fit with ½-inch overlap. Pin with small skewers or round toothpicks. Grill, turning from time to time with tongs, until the bacon is cooked the way you like it. Serve hot.

*I assume here, and elsewhere throughout this book, that a "serving" is one steak per person.

Be warned that the bacon will drip and cause serious fires. It's best to stand by the grill while cooking, tongs in hand, and move the tenderloins about to avoid scorching the meat.

FRENCH PROVENÇAL HERBED STEAKS

I like this recipe because it gives me control of the herbs *after* the steaks have been cooked. I don't care for much herb flavor on medium-rare beef, but I realize that others do. If the steak is marinated for hours with herbs in the mix, it is difficult to control the flavor if it be too much or too little. In any case, this recipe has been adapted from *French Farm House Cookbook,* by Susan Herrmann Loomis. The ingredients list calls for ¼ cup of mixed fresh herbs. These can include summer savory, thyme, and rosemary, or you can add your own choice—and there are dozens of suitable herbs, including half a dozen basils, for those who think they can tell the difference in the finished steaks. The recipe calls for sea salt, of which I heartily approve, and there are several sorts available today. If you have a coarse salt (as well you should), grind it in a mill, like peppercorns, or crush it in a mortar and pestle.

4 T-bones
½ cup chopped fresh herbs
  (see note above)
2 tablespoons olive oil (divided)

2 cloves garlic, peeled
  and minced
sea salt and freshly
  ground black pepper

Rig for grilling over charcoal or wood coals. When the coals are quite hot, brush the steaks on both sides with about half the olive oil. Grill the steaks for 4 or 5 minutes on both sides until medium rare, or done to your liking. When you turn the steaks, sprinkle them with salt and pepper. While they finish cooking, mix the herbs, garlic, and the rest of the olive oil, along with a little salt. Place the steaks on heated plates and spread each with part of the herb mixture. Serve hot.

KOREAN STEAK

Most Asian recipes call for cutting the steaks into thin strips, as in a stir-fry. Here's a different way. I enjoy it for a change, served as a lunch or a light dinner. Note that these steaks are quite thin and difficult to slice without special equipment. You might ask your butcher to slice them for you. The recipe calls for two prepared pastes, both of which can be purchased in Korean food stores. The *gouchu jang* paste, a standard seasoning in Korean cooking, is made with rice, fermented soybean cake, hot chili, and other ingredients. The *denjang* paste, also standard in Korean cooking, is made from fermented soybeans. According to *The Korean Kitchen,* by Copeland Marks, *denjang* matures like old wine and can be kept for as long as 30 years. Good stuff. The sesame oil used in the recipe is made from burnt seeds and is used as a flavoring. Do not use the sesame cooking oil.

THE MEAT AND WRAPPER

8 thin ribeye steaks
(¼ inch thick)
8 large lettuce leaves,
romaine or Boston

2 tablespoons *denjang*
paste
1 tablespoon *gouchu jang*
paste

THE MARINADE

2 green onions, chopped
3 cloves garlic, minced
1 tablespoon soy sauce
1 tablespoon rice wine
or dry vermouth

2 teaspoons sugar
1 teaspoon sesame oil
(Asian-style)
½ teaspoon freshly ground
black pepper

Mix the marinade ingredients in a nonmetallic container. Add the steaks, tossing about to coat all sides of the meat. Marinate for 2 to 4 hours. Rig for grilling over hot charcoal or wood coals. Make a sauce by combining the *denjang* and *gouchu jang* pastes; set aside at room temperature. When the coals are very hot, broil the steaks about 4 inches from the heat for about 1 minute on each side, or until done medium rare. Do not overcook. Lay out the lettuce leaves, smearing each one to taste with the prepared hot sauce. Place a steak on each leaf, roll with the lettuce on the outside, and eat out of hand.

TERIYAKI RIBEYES

These steaks are best cooked whole, then sliced before serving. But I like to serve whole ribeyes, letting each diner carve his own. With some cuts, however, it may be best to carve before serving. The marinade ingredients make enough to soak four ribeyes. Adjust the measures for more or less meat, but exact measures aren't critical.

4 ribeyes	**2 tablespoons sugar**
¼ cup soy sauce	**1 tablespoon freshly grated**
¼ cup peanut oil	** gingerroot**
¼ cup sake or perhaps	**2 cloves garlic, minced**
** dry red wine**	**freshly ground black pepper**

Mix all the marinade ingredients in a nonmetallic container. Add the steaks, turning about to coat all sides, and marinate for about 5 hours at room temperature, or longer in the refrigerator. Rig for grilling over hot charcoal, wood, gas, or electric heat, putting the meat 4 inches from the heat. Grill for 6 or 7 minutes, or until done to your liking, turning several times. Serve hot.

20-GAUGE RIBEYES

One of my favorite steak dinners came about without a plan. Upon learning that I had to feed two of my teenage sons, I sent them to the grocery store, a few blocks away, for steaks and mushrooms. I also told them to pick up a bag of mixed salad at the produce counter, looking closely for fresh lettuce without any brown spots. They returned with four juicy ribeyes—not three. For balance, they got four huge portabellos. All the ribeyes, they said, were packaged two up, and it never occurred to them to ask the butcher for three. The salad they forgot, they said. Anyhow, I cooked the steaks and mushrooms on a built-in stovetop electric grill, and they turned out to be memorable. The boys split the extra steak and portabello. Here's my "recipe." For information on the 20-Gauge sauce, see chapter 12.

ribeye steaks (with an extra one or two)	**huge potatoes (cooked separately)**
Myron's 20-Gauge wild game sauce	**no salad**
portabellos, whole	**butter**
	salt and freshly ground black pepper

Grind some peppercorns over the steaks, setting the mill on coarse, or use some freshly cracked pepper. Rub the pepper into the steaks with the palm of your hand. Brush the steaks on both sides with 20-Gauge. Stack the steaks and set aside for 30 minutes or so, while the potatoes are cooking. Heat the grill and grease the rack. Mix and heat a basting sauce, using half butter and half 20-Gauge. Cook the steaks and portabellos for 4 or 5 minutes on each side, until medium rare, basting several times.

STEAK M. F. K. FISHER

In her book *An Alphabet for Gourmets,* M. F. K. Fisher, my kind of woman, said, "This recipe is anyone's for the taking." Well, thank you ma'am. I like the recipe, the spirit, and the menu, to be discussed below.

1 large sirloin, 2 or preferably 3 inches thick	1 cup melted butter
3 cups good red wine	¾ cup good olive oil (divided)
2 cups mixed chopped scallions, celery, green pepper, parsley, and (if available) fresh basil	¾ cup good soy sauce (divided)
	6 cloves garlic

Mix the butter, wine, and chopped green stuff in a saucepan and simmer over very low heat for about an hour, stirring often with a wooden spoon; keep it warm. Peel the garlic cloves and cut in half. Rub the steak thoroughly with the garlic halves, covering every inch. Place the steak into a shallow dish. Rub the upside with about ¼ cup of soy sauce. Leave at room temperature for 30 minutes. Turn the steak and rub the other side with another ¼ cup of soy sauce. Let stand a few minutes, then pour in about half the olive oil. Turn several times while you rig for grilling over charcoal. Place the steak on a greased rack about 4 inches above the coals. Cook it for about 20 minutes, turning from time to time (note that the meat is quite close to the coals and must be turned often, after the first few minutes, to avoid burning) and moving it about on the rack to avoid fires in the grill, or until medium rare. A 3-inch steak may take a little longer. Do not overcook. Pour the hot sauce into a baking pan or other suitable flat container. Add the rest of the olive oil and soy sauce, mixing well. Bring to a boil, perhaps on the grill. Carefully place the hot steak onto the pan and remove from the heat. Turn the steak to coat all sides with the sauce. Slice the steak into ½-inch slices, letting each one soak up some sauce before serving.

As Ms. Fisher said, "This somewhat primeval dish is easy to prepare, once practiced. I always serve it generously, with equally generous baskets of slightly toasted sourdough bread (for sopping), piles of fresh watercress in wooden bowls, platters of thickly sliced tomatoes (innocent of anything but a possible sprinkling of chopped fresh basil), and ample Tipo Red or ale. I used to have cheeses later, for what was left of the bread, but I have found that a basket of cool fresh fruit and cups of strong 'Louisiana' coffee are more welcome to the pleasantly stimulated and at the same time surfeited diners." I agree, except that I prefer a touch of sea salt, and no basil, on my sliced tomatoes. Louisiana coffee, by the way, is part chicory root and part coffee bean, well toasted before grinding. I drink a pot of the coffee, strongly brewed, every morning. The mixed grounds are available in some markets under several brand names. Of course, I will allow any kind of coffee to be served, but I insist that it be brewed from freshly ground coffee beans. The aroma is part of it. The caffeine, too.

KANSAS CITY STEAK, INDIRECT-STYLE

If the book *Kansas City Barbecue* is a reliable indicator, the boys in this beef-eating neck of the woods love to cook on a large covered grill, either gas or charcoal. The method is to build the fire (or light the burners) only on one side. When the fire and grid are quite hot, the steaks are seared for 1 minute—30 seconds on each side—and then moved to the "cold" side. The cover is lowered and the steaks are cooked for 7 to 10 minutes, depending on their thickness. This recipe, by the way, works best with thicker steaks—1½ to 2 inches.

I like these steaks, but I'll have to be honest. I prefer to cook 'em over high heat all the way, without the hood. But suit yourself. The ingredients list below calls for a gin sauce, but other sauces can be used. The gin, however, really does go nicely with red meat—and especially with venison. In fact, gin is flavored with the juniper berry, which is a popular spice among wild game chefs. (See the juniper sauce recipe in chapter 12.)

1 sirloin steak, 2 inches thick	**¼ cup good gin**
½ cup melted butter	**salt and freshly ground black pepper**

Rig for grilling over a wood fire, charcoal, or gas heat. While waiting, rub the steak with salt and pepper and leave at room temperature. When the grill is hot, sear the steak for 30 seconds on each side, using tongs, and using tongs, move it to the cold side of the grill. Lower the hood and cook for 10 minutes. While waiting, mix the butter and gin in a saucepan. Heat but do not boil. Turn the steak and cook for another 7 minutes, or until medium rare. Place the steak onto a heated platter and set it in the middle of the table. Seat the guests. Using a long match, light the gin sauce and pour it, flaming, over the steak. Carve up the steak and eat at once.

LIBBY HILLMAN'S GOURMET STEAK

In *Gourmet Cookbook,* first published back in 1963, Libby Hillman detailed a slightly different method of grilling a thick steak on a large covered grill. It is, in short, exactly backward from the Kansas City method. Try it with a thick sirloin or T-bones.

sirloin or other steaks   **soy sauce**
   cut 2 inches thick   **Worcestershire sauce**

Build a hot charcoal fire on one side of the grill. While waiting for the coals to heat up, lightly sprinkle the steaks on each side with soy sauce and Worcestershire sauce. Leave at room temperature until the coals are hot. Place the steaks on the grill well away from the heat. Close the cover and cook for about 45 minutes, turning from time to time. Add more fuel to the fire, if needed, and finish the steaks directly over the hot coals, grilling each side until it is nicely browned. Serve immediately. Note that no salt or pepper is added to the steak before or during cooking, but a salt shaker and a pepper mill should be on the table.

WYOMING BUFFALO COOKOUT STEAKS

The sauce made below, an old Wyoming recipe, is especially good for basting grilled bison steaks. It can also be used to advantage on beef and venison steaks.

10 pounds buffalo ribeye or T-bone steaks	2 tablespoons Accent (optional)
12 ounces tomato sauce	1 tablespoon garlic powder
2 cups olive oil	1 tablespoon black pepper
2 cups dry red wine	1 tablespoon dried sweet basil
2 tablespoons salt	½ tablespoon dried oregano

Put all the ingredients except the meat in a large Mason jar, stirring or shaking to mix well. Rig for grilling over hot coals. When the coals are very hot, quickly sear the steaks on both sides. Then grill one side for about 3 or 4 minutes. Turn and baste heavily from the Mason jar. Grill for 3 or 4 minutes. Turn and baste heavily, grilling for 1 minute. Turn, baste, and serve hot. For best results, the meat should be rare or medium rare. The exact cooking times depend on the thickness of the meat and the heat. Do not overcook.

Note: If you don't want to cook 10 pounds of meat, reduce the measure of sauce ingredients accordingly or refrigerate some of the sauce for another cookout. It's good on grilled pork steaks and cutlets.

LAMB STEAKS WITH SUMAC

The best sumac, according to the ancient Roman epicures, comes from Syria. Maybe so, but the spice is enjoyed in many parts of the Middle East. The spice in powder form—apparently ground sumac berries—is available in some ethnic and gourmet food shops and by mail order. Sumac also grows wild in great profusion in many parts of North America and should be more widely used in this country. The Native Americans used it to make Indian lemonade, and the early settlers used sumac as a substitute for lemon juice. I use wild sumac for cooking purposes, in spite of admonitions from TV chefs, one of whom (billed as the Frugal Gourmet) said, "Do not pick sumac from your backyard, but rather buy this wonderful spice in any Middle Eastern market. Our domestic sumac could make you ill, but the sumac from the Holy Land will delight you." I won't try to defend American sumac in full, but the guy was probably intimidated because of the term "poison sumac," which has white berries. All species of edible sumac, such as staghorn, have red berries. Readers who want to eat bravely should know that sumac berries should not be rinsed (as is recommended in some books) before grinding. The wonderful flavor—malic acid—is on the surface of many tiny hairs that grow around the berry. Washing the berry will remove the good stuff. (That's why the berries should not be harvested soon after a heavy rain.)

Instead of grinding the berries into a spice, it's best to rinse the whole cluster in cold water. Then throw the berries out and strain the water. The infusion makes a very good drink (Indian lemonade), sweetened with a little sugar. It can also be boiled, concentrating the flavor. I prefer to use the liquid for cooking, but the recipe below calls for the Syrian sumac, meaning the stuff sold at high prices in Middle Eastern markets. If you do make a sumac infusion, however, use it to taste and omit the lemon juice.

2 pounds lamb chops or lamb T-bones	**2 tablespoons olive oil**
juice of 2 lemons	**salt and freshly ground black pepper**
2 tablespoons sumac powder	

Mix the lemon juice, olive oil, sumac power, salt, and pepper. Brush the chops on both sides with the mixture. Set them aside for an hour, stacking one atop the other. Rig for grilling over charcoal, placing the rack about 4 inches above the coals. Grill on one side for 3 minutes. Turn and baste. Grill the other side for 2 or 3 minutes, or until done. Turn again and baste. Serve hot, along with grilled eggplant, a green salad, and rice pilaf.

Note: Hunters lucky enough to bag a bighorn sheep should try this recipe.

JAMES BEARD'S TURKISH MUTTON CHOPS

Although mutton is not readily available in most parts of this country, it damn well ought to be. It's great stuff for grilling, if you like the taste of meat. For this recipe, use chops about 1½ inches to 2 inches thick. I like to allow two chops per person, but one will do if you've got plenty of rice and Turkish eggplant, soused with olive oil and grilled alongside the meat. For this recipe—and for so much more—I am in debt to the late James Beard, a champion of mutton.

4 mutton chops	2 cloves garlic, minced
¼ cup butter	2 teaspoons chopped fresh mint
¼ cup minced pine nuts	salt and freshly ground
¼ cup chopped fresh parsley	black pepper

Cut a small pocket in the center of each chop. Mix and mash together the garlic, pine nuts, parsley, mint, and butter, preferably with a mortar and pestle. Spoon about a quarter of the mixture into each chop. Grill rather slowly over charcoal, 6 or 8 inches from the heat, until medium rare. Sprinkle with salt and pepper to taste and serve hot (the great Grillmaster says) with broiled eggplant and broiled tomatoes, along with a red wine and, for dessert, ripe mangos or melon.

GOOD OL' BOY PORK CHOPS

Here's an easy way to grill tasty pork chops. Use fresh pork, preferably T-bones, from 1½ to 2 inches thick. Your butcher may have to cut them for you on special order, or you can cut your own from a pork loin if you have a meat saw.

thick pork chops
zesty Italian salad dressing
lemon-pepper seasoning salt

Rig for grilling over charcoal, placing the rack 6 to 8 inches above the heat. When the coals are hot, baste the chops with zesty Italian dressing and grill for about 15 minutes on each side, turning and basting lightly from time to time. Cook until the centers of the chops are no longer pink—but still juicy. The exact time depends on the thickness of the chops and the heat. If in doubt, use an instant-reading meat thermometer, cooking until the chops are 150 degrees in the center; then let them coast a little before serving. A few minutes before removing the chops from the grill, sprinkle them lightly with lemon-pepper seasoning salt.

Variation I: Marinate the chops (thick ones) for an hour or longer in a mixture of 1 cup soy sauce, 1 tablespoon prepared mustard, and ½ tablespoon black pepper. Cook as directed above, basting lightly with bacon drippings.

Variation II: Cook the chops as directed above, basting from time to time with a mixture of 1 cup melted butter, ¼ cup freshly squeezed lemon juice, and 2 tablespoons honey.

Variation III: If you want more smoke flavor, add some wet wood chips (or, preferably, chips or chunks of green hardwood such as hickory or oak) around the charcoal and close the hood of the grill while cooking.

HAM STEAKS WITH PINEAPPLE

Center-cut "cured" ham steaks, from 1 to 2 inches thick, are delicious when grilled over charcoal. These are cut from the regular supermarket hams, not from the salt-cured hard hams. Ham steaks need nothing added, but I like to baste lightly with a mixture of brown sugar and prepared mustard during the last few minutes of grilling. Pineapple slices can be grilled and served atop the ham, but I prefer grilled pineapple quarters, (chapter 11). In any case, these modern hams are almost foolproof on the grill. The salt-cured country hams, however, require special handling and should be soaked or freshened overnight in several changes of water to remove some of the salt and to add moisture to the dry meat, which will actually expand.

TURKEY STEAKS WITH POMEGRANATE SAUCE

Here's another dish from the Middle East and the Caucasus. It is made with the aid of pomegranate juice, which has a wonderful flavor. Bottled pomegranate syrup, or molasses, is available in ethnic food stores, but homemade is much better and has a better color. I have my own pomegranate trees, and the fruits can be purchased in supermarkets in the fall of the year. Remove the seeds from the pomegranate, throwing out the pith and rind. (Be warned that pomegranate juice will stain your clothes.) Squeeze the juice out of the seeds and reduce it in a saucepan until you have a thin or thick syrup, as you like it. Add sugar if you want it.

The turkey steaks used in this recipe are cut from the breast, across the bone. They should be cut between 1 and 2 inches thick. I can sometimes buy them precut at the supermarket, but as often as not I have the butcher slice a whole turkey breast for me, fresh or frozen. The same recipe can also be used for pork and alligator steaks.

turkey steaks	**butter**
pomegranate syrup	**salt and pepper**

Rig for grilling over wood coals, charcoal, gas, or electric heat, adjusting the rack 3 or 4 inches above the heat source. In a saucepot, melt the butter and mix in the pomegranate syrup. Add the pomegranate syrup slowly, tasting as you go, until you get the intensity you want. I like it quite tart. Grill the turkey steaks for 3 minutes, then turn, baste with butter-pomegranate mixture, and sprinkle with salt and pepper. Grill for 3 minutes or so, turn, and baste. Cook until done, turning every 2 minutes. Baste lightly with each turn. Serve hot with grilled vegetables, grilled fruits, skewered button mushrooms (chapter 11), and rice pilaf.

Warning: If you use a sweetened pomegranate syrup, do not baste until the turkey steaks are almost done. If you do, the syrup will burn. As an alternate recipe, save the sweetened pomegranate syrup to pour (sparingly) over the cooked turkey. Before grilling the turkey, baste the steaks lightly with sour cream and let them rest at room temperature while the fire is getting hot.

STEAKS IN THE SKILLET

2

I ENJOY COOKING STEAKS in a skillet, if I don't have to feed many people. It's a hands-on kind of cooking, best performed at the kitchen stove while the guests, seated at the table and ready, sip a glass of wine and nosh on a little cheese and while the spouse tosses a green salad and butters the bread.

The best skillet steaks—ribeyes and boned loin cuts—need no marinade before being cooked, especially if you like the flavor of beefsteak. The tougher cuts require more handling and longer cooking, preferably au jus, helped along with a little beef stock or wine, or both. Many of the recipes below call for a skillet sauce, made quickly after the steaks have been cooked.

In any case, it's best to use heavy-duty skillets. I prefer cast iron. Electric skillets will do, especially for recipes that require long simmering. The skillets with a ribbed bottom are not suited for cooking the recipes in this chapter, partly because they drain away the good juices. I have decided to discuss these in a separate chapter, along with the waffle-iron-type electric grills, and the larger ribbed griddles and other branding-iron tactics.

STEAK AU POIVRE

For this simple but regal dish I prefer to use a porterhouse or T-bone
large enough to fill the skillet, but several tenderloins cut 2 inches thick
and butterflied will also work, as will New York strips or ribeyes. (All the
various steaks are discussed in chapter 10.) For greasing the skillet, I normally use beef fat rendered from the steak trimmings. Olive oil will do.

1 or 2 very good steaks,	**1 tablespoon rendered beef fat**
1 inch thick	**or olive oil**
½ cup light cream	**freshly cracked black pepper**
¼ cup cognac	**salt**

Grind some black pepper, using a coarse setting on your mill, or
crack some peppercorns between wax paper, perhaps using the
smooth end of a meat mallet. Sprinkle both sides of the steak liberally with pepper, pressing it into the meat. Let stand for an hour. Set
the table and get everything ready for serving so that the steak can
be served hot. Heat the fat or olive oil in a cast-iron skillet over
medium-high heat. When you are ready to cook, sprinkle both sides
of the steak with salt. Cook for about 4 minutes on each side, or until
medium rare. The inside should be very juicy but should not run red;
the outside, crusty and richly browned. Remove the steaks to a heated serving platter or heavy plate. Quickly reduce the heat to the skillet. Slowly add the cognac to the pan drippings, stirring as you go
with a wooden spoon and scraping up any crusty bits from the bottom of the skillet. Stir in the cream, shaking the skillet as you go.
Bring to a light boil, then quickly reduce the heat and simmer for a
minute or two. Pour the sauce over the steak and serve at once, along
with sautéed mushrooms, asparagus or French-cut beans (or other
vegetables), a baked Idaho potato or two, and a hot crusty bread.

UBALDI ON STEAK AU POIVRE

Jack Ubaldi, founder of the Florence Prime Meat Market in New
York City and coauthor of *Jack Ubaldi's Meat Book,* uses a mixture of

black and white peppercorns, mixed and crushed with a rolling pin. The crushed peppercorns are worked into the surface with the palm of the hand. Then the steaks are rested in the refrigerator for 2 hours. Next, he browns the steaks on both sides in a skillet, using a mixture of butter and oil, and removes them to a warm platter or plate. The fat is removed from the skillet, replaced by 1 tablespoon of new butter. He cooks 2 tablespoons of chopped shallots for a minute or two. Now he deglazes the pan with ½ cup of beef stock and a jigger of cognac. After reducing the sauce by half, he removes the skillet and stirs in 3 tablespoons of soft butter, a little at a time. Then he tastes for seasoning (presumably adding salt or pepper, if needed) and pours the sauce over the steaks. He serves the steaks with french fries, along with a salad of endive and watercress.

FLAMED PEPPER STEAK

Here's a good dish to cook whenever you want to put on a show, perhaps while courting. But it's also simple enough for camp cookery, where the skillet is likely to catch on fire anyway.

tender steak (cooked to order for each person)	**freshly ground or cracked black pepper**
	salt
warmed brandy	**butter**

Sprinkle the steak liberally on both sides with coarsely ground or cracked pepper, pressing it into the meat. Let stand for an hour. When you are ready to cook, heat a little butter in your favorite skillet. Cook the steak for 4 minutes, turn it, sprinkle the cooked side with salt, and sizzle the other side for 3 or 4 minutes, or until medium rare. Pour a little warmed brandy (not quite ¼ cup) into the skillet, with some going directly over the steak. Then flame the whole works. Put the steak onto a heated platter. Swirl the pan juices and pour over the steak.

IRISH STEAKS

I like to cook this dish with a porterhouse or big T-bone, doing, of course, one steak at a time. If you prefer, or have the need, try two ribeyes or New York strip steaks side by side, snug in the skillet. Oh, I sometimes fantasize on eating these steaks by candlelight with a hearty Irish lass with red, red hair and deep blue eyes.

1 porterhouse, 1 to 1½ inches thick, or 2 twin ribeyes	heavy cream
garlic butter	salt and freshly ground pepper
Irish whiskey, warmed	watercress or parsley

A few minutes before cooking, rub each steak on both sides with garlic butter. Heat a skillet or griddle over high heat. (Add no grease to the skillet.) Cook the steak for 4 or 5 minutes on each side, or until done to your liking. Pour in a jigger or two of warm Irish whiskey and flame. Place the steak on a heated plate or serving platter. Add a little cream to the skillet and scrape up any bits that have stuck to the bottom. Simmer for a few minutes, then pour over the steak. Sprinkle with salt and pepper to taste. Serve hot, garnished with watercress or parsley. Serve with new Irish potatoes and other vegetables of your choice, along with a loaf of Irish soda bread.

After eating, finish the evening beside the fireplace with a glass of Irish coffee, one of the most wonderful treats to come out of the Western world. Make it only with very strong coffee, good Irish whiskey, and a little brown sugar, topped, of course, with real whipped cream, as directed in chapter 11.

CARPETBAG STEAKS

The Australians cook a skillet steak with the aid of an oyster or two. Since I love oysters on the half shell, and have a steady supply in season, I cook this one several times a year, sometimes with with game steaks. When using venison, the recipe works best with a loin steak about 1½ inches thick and with small, freshly shucked oysters.

loin steaks, 1½ inches thick
small fresh oysters
butter

chopped fresh parsley
   or watercress
salt and pepper

When you shuck the oysters, save all the juice—and do not under any circumstances *wash* the oysters (as directed in some modern cookbooks). Cut a pocket in each steak, working from the side and keeping the slit as small as possible. I use a very sharp blade of my pocketknife or a fillet knife. Stuff the steak with an oyster or two. Skewer the slit shut with a toothpick toed in from the side so that the steaks can be turned in the skillet. Heat a little butter in a skillet—about 1 tablespoon per steak. Cook the steak for 4 or 5 minutes, turn, and cook for 4 or 5 minutes on the other side. (Two steaks can be cooked at a time, but increase the butter a little.) Place the steak on a heated plate, salt and pepper to taste. Heat a little more butter in the skillet, add the chopped parsley, swirl in some oyster juice, and scrape up any pan dredgings, working toward a sauce. Add the rest of the oyster juice and reduce until the sauce has thickened. Pour the sauce over the steak and serve at once.

STEAK DIANA

This dish, fittingly named, works better with tender venison steaks from along the backbone. Tenderloin of elk or moose can be sliced into 1-inch steaks, or smaller back straps from whitetail or other smaller deer can be butterflied. If you don't have any beef or venison stock at hand, stir a bouillon cube into a cup of hot water.

4 small steaks, 1 inch thick
½ cup chopped shallots
¼ cup beef or venison stock
¼ cup cognac
2 tablespoons olive oil

1 tablespoon butter
1 tablespoon Dijon mustard
1 tablespoon chopped fresh chives
juice of ½ lemon
salt and freshly ground black pepper

Heat the olive oil in a large cast-iron skillet over medium-high heat. Salt and pepper the steaks on both sides. Sauté the steaks for 4 minutes on each side, or until medium rare. (Or rare if you prefer.) Do not overcook. Remove the steaks to a heated platter. Add the butter to the skillet. Sauté the shallots and chives for 3 or 4 minutes. Stir in the stock, cognac, mustard, lemon juice, salt, and pepper. Cook for 2 or 3 minutes, stirring as you go with a wooden spoon. Pour the sauce over the steaks. Serve hot with asparagus, morels shamelessly sautéed in plenty of butter, crusty bread, and good red wine, pausing just long enough to toast Diana, ancient Roman goddess of the hunt.

Note: Some steak Diana recipes call for a little sherry or port in addition to the cognac. If you are so inclined, cut back 1 tablespoon of cognac and add 1 tablespoon sherry or port (preferably). Note also that some people call this recipe steak Diane.

SKILLET STEAK ACCORDING TO HERTER

A man of firm and sometimes outrageous opinions, George Leonard Herter, coauthor of *Bull Cook and Authentic Historical Recipes and Practices,* is fond of cooking a steak in beef suet—considered poison in some health food circles—and then swabbing it in butter before serving. His thinking is that beef suet has a high smoke point, permitting the cook to get it quite hot in a skillet without actually burning it. This in turn allows the cook to sear the steak nicely on both sides, sealing in all the fatty juices and blood. I have to confirm that such a steak, cooked medium rare, is indeed tasty. This hot-cooking method works best in a cast-iron skillet, but not in Teflon. And be warned that some expensive ceramic-clad skillets may crack when subjected to very high heat. Beef suet, by the way, is simply a choice beef cooking fat. I almost always use beef fat trimmed from ribeyes or T-bones.

ribeye or T-bone steaks **salt and freshly ground black pepper**
beef suet or fat **butter**

Heat enough beef suet to cover the bottom of the skillet by a depth of ⅛ inch. (If you fry out the beef fat, cut it into small dice, then fry out the grease, saving the cracklings to serve over the salad or sprinkle over the mashed potatoes.) Heat the beef fat just short of the smoking point. Salt and pepper each steak on both sides, then sear it on both sides. Sizzle it until done (medium rare, I say) and place it on paper towels or, better, a flattened brown bag, turning to blot both sides, and quickly put it onto a heated plate. Add a pat or two of butter and serve hot.

RUSSIAN STEAKS

Try this Russian recipe with ribeyes or perhaps butterflied tender-loin. The wild-game lover fortunate enough to have bear—an old favorite in Russia and northern Europe—should use loin steaks. The recipe is best cooked with the aid of two cast-iron skillets. Be sure to use clarified butter (chapter 12); regular butter will brown too much. Also, remember that the Russians often pound steaks and pork chops with a meat mallet before cooking them.

2 ribeyes, 1 inch thick,
   lightly pounded
2 large chicken eggs
¼ cup clarified butter

minced fresh dill weed
salt and freshly ground
   black pepper

Salt and pepper each steak on both sides. Heat most of the butter in a skillet. Cook the steaks for a few minutes on each side until medi-um rare. In a separate skillet, using the rest of the butter, fry the eggs sunny-side up. Put the steaks onto heated serving plates, top with a fried egg, and pour some juice from the meat pan over all. Sprinkle lightly with dill. Serve with crusty hot bread, boiled new potatoes, and a green vegetable.

OLD DOMINION STEAK

Housekeeping in Old Virginia, a good book published back in 1879, had some surprisingly modern advice on cooking steaks in a skillet (called broiling by the author, but in this book "broiling" means cooking in the oven under a heat source). Anyhow, here's a quote: "For steak, nothing is so nice as tenderloin or porterhouse steak. I take this occasion to protest against the unwholesome custom of frying steak in lard. When inconvenient to broil, it may be deliciously cooked by being first beaten till tender, then laid in a hot frying pan, closely covered, and cooked without lard or butter, in its own juices. When scorched brown on both sides, but not hard, remove the pan from the fire, pepper and salt the steak, and put a large tablespoonful of fresh butter on it. Press this in with a knife and fork, turning the steak, so that each side may absorb the butter. Serve on a hot dish. The whole process will not consume five minutes. Some persons think it best to add the salt after the steak is done, though many good housekeepers salt and pepper the steak before broiling it. Beefsteak should be cooked rare; it is a great mistake to cook it till hard and indigestible."

Another recipe in the same book says, "Take a thin, long-handled frying-pan, put it on the stove and heat it quite hot. In this put the pieces of steak previously pounded, but do not put a particle of butter in the frying-pan and do not salt the steak. Allow the steak to merely glaze over and then turn it quickly to the other side, turning it several times in this manner, until it is done. Four minutes is sufficient for cooking. When done, lay it on the platter, previously warmed; butter and salt, and set a moment in the hot oven. Allow the steak to heat but a moment on each side [while cooking in the skillet]; this helps it to retain all its sweet juices, and putting on the salt at the last moment, after it is on the platter, draws out its juices."

CUBAN TENDERLOINS

Here's an old recipe from Cuba. The tenderloins are cut 1½ inches thick, and the overall sizes depend on which part of the tenderloin they are cut from. I will want two of these, but one will do if I've got plenty of go-withs. If you have a length of tenderloin and plan to cut your own steaks, consider butterflying segments on the small end.

4 to 6 tenderloins,   1 tablespoon chopped fresh
  1½ inches thick   parsley or cilantro
½ cup clarified butter   juice of 1 lemon
1 medium to large onion,   salt and freshly ground
  chopped   black pepper to taste
2 cloves garlic, minced

Mix lemon juice, onion, garlic, parsley, salt, and pepper in a non-metallic container. Add the steaks, tossing to coat all sides, and marinate for 1 hour. Remove the steaks and reserve the marinade. Heat about half the butter in a heavy skillet large enough to hold the steaks. Cook for 4 or 5 minutes on each side, or until the steaks are done to your liking. Medium rare is my recommendation. Place the steaks on a heated serving platter. Heat the rest of the butter in the skillet and add the marinade. Bring to a boil, lower the heat, and cook for 2 or 3 minutes. Pour the sauce over the steaks and serve hot.

    Note: If you have a sour orange (Seville) at hand, try it instead of the lemon. Double the measure of juice for the marinade, and increase the cooking times for the sauce.

BRAZILIAN STEAKS

You'll need some strong, freshly brewed coffee for this recipe. It will help to fill the kitchen with the aroma of freshly roasted and ground coffee beans.

4 ribeyes   2 tablespoons olive oil
1 cup strong black coffee   ½ teaspoon garlic juice
½ cup chopped scallions   salt and freshly ground
  with part of green tops   black pepper
¼ cup butter

Heat the olive oil in a cast-iron skillet over high heat. Sear the steaks on each side, then lower the heat to medium high. Cook for 2 or 3 minutes on each side, or until the steaks are medium rare. Remove the steaks to a heated platter. Quickly melt the butter in the skillet and add the garlic juice. Reduce the heat to medium. Add the coffee, stirring with a wooden spoon to scrape up any steak bits from the bottom. Cook on high heat, stirring as you go, until the mixture is reduced by half. Add a little salt and pepper to taste. Pour the sauce over the steaks and sprinkle the tops with the green onions. Serve hot. Feeds four.

JACKLEG COUNTRY STEAKS

Every camp cook worth his salt has a recipe for country steak, sometimes called chicken-fried steak. Typically, the meat is sprinkled with salt, pepper, and flour, then beaten until tender with a meat mallet, the edge of a heavy plate, or the mouth of a heavy-duty bottle. For best results, the steaks are turned a few times and sprinkled with flour between each beating. Finally, the steaks are fried in hot grease until nicely browned. Then they are removed and most of the grease is poured out of the skillet. A little flour is added and stirred about until it turns brown. Water or stock is poured into the skillet, stirring all the while, until a nice gravy comes. The steaks are served hot, with the gravy spooned over biscuit halves, mashed potatoes, or rice.

I sometimes go a step farther, especially if the steaks are a little tough. After making a rather thin gravy, I fit the steaks back into the skillet, cover tightly, and simmer for 30 minutes or longer, until the steaks are tender enough to cut with a fork. It may be necessary to add a little water and turn the steaks from time to time.

Many people use round beefsteak for this and similar recipes, but I can get by with venison steaks made from cross sections of the hind leg. If properly made and not overcooked, these steaks are always good in camp, or for any big breakfast on a cold morning before a hunt.

CREOLE CHUCK STEAKS

Chuck steaks can be cooked successfully in a skillet, and they are very tasty if they are simmered in gravy or perhaps condensed mushroom soup diluted with a little red wine. I especially like this Creole-type recipe, cooked in a large cast-iron skillet.

large chuck steak about
  1 inch thick
1 can beef broth
  (14-ounce size)
8 ounces button mushrooms,
  sliced
2 large ripe tomatoes, diced
1 large onion, cut lengthwise
  into boat-shaped pieces
1 green bell pepper, seeded
  and cut lengthwise into strips

1 small green jalapeño, seeded
  and cut into strips
¼ cup olive oil or lard
2 teaspoons cornstarch
flour
salt and freshly ground
  black pepper
¼ teaspoon cayenne
  (or to taste)

Salt and pepper the steak on both sides, then sprinkle with flour. Beat with a meat mallet or the edge of a heavy saucer or plate. Turn the steak, sprinkle on a little more flour, and beat again. Heat the oil or lard in a large, heavy skillet. Sear the steak for a minute or two on both sides, turning once. Add the mushrooms, onion, and peppers. Reduce the heat to medium low and cook for 10 minutes, moving the contents around with a wooden spoon, making sure all the vegetables touch bottom from time to time. Turn the steak. Add the tomatoes and cook for another 5 minutes. Add the beef broth and and cayenne. Cover and simmer on very low for 30 to 40 minutes, or until the steak is tender. Move the steak to a heated platter, or cut it and place serving portions on individual heated plates. Quickly, mix a little water into the cornstarch until you have a paste. Stir this into the skillet mixture and cook, stirring as you go, until the sauce thickens and becomes bubbly. Spoon the sauce over the steak. Eat at once, preferably with French bread and rice. The chunky vegetables in the sauce negate the need for side dishes, but a tropical fruit salad would be nice, especially if you go heavy on the cayenne.

VENISON STEAK WITH ONION GRAVY

This recipe can be used with any good venison steak, perhaps a round of hind leg, without the aid of a marinade. I sometimes cook it with beef eye of round, which is a pretty but tough little cut of meat. If you don't have any beef stock on hand, use a bouillon cube dissolved in hot water.

2 pounds venison steaks,
  ½ inch thick
1 cup cooking oil
1 cup beef or game stock
1 medium to large onion,
  minced

3 cloves garlic, minced
1 teaspoon Pickapeppa
  sauce or Worcestershire
flour
salt and pepper

Heat the oil in a skillet. Salt and pepper the steaks, dust them with flour, and brown them on both sides, cooking in two or more batches if necessary. Drain the steaks. Pour most of the oil out of the skillet, leaving about 2 tablespoons. Sauté the onion for 5 minutes. Add the garlic, cooking for a few more minutes. Stir in and brown 1 tablespoon flour, stirring constantly with a wooden spoon. Add the stock, stirring well, and enough water to make a thin gravy. Stir in the Pickapeppa. Return the steaks to the skillet. Cover, lower the heat, and simmer for 2 hours, or until very tender. Add a little water from time to time, and turn the steaks to keep the bottom from burning. Serve hot, spooning the gravy over rice or mashed potatoes. I like this onion gravy for breakfast over biscuit halves.

L. L. BEAN'S VENISON STEAK

L. L. Bean was a jackleg skillet cook, at least in camp, and he has rather firm opinions on the way to cook trout and other outdoor foods. In this venison recipe (which was set forth in his book *Hunting, Fishing, and Camping* and rehashed by other hands in *The L. L. Bean Game and Fish Cookbook*) Bean uses no grease in the skillet. If you try his method, use any good venison steak, cut 1½ inches thick. I recommend butterflied loin steaks, but hind-leg rounds will also work. Do not overcook.

venison steak
butter
salt and pepper

Closely trim any fat from the edges of the steak. Heat the skillet over a hot fire. Sear the steak on one side, then turn and sear the other side. Reduce the heat and cook the steak for about 10 minutes, turning from time to time, or until rare or medium rare. Do not overcook venison. Place the steak onto a heated plate, spread with butter, sprinkle with salt and pepper, and serve hot.

WYOMING ELK STEAK

One of my favorite regional culinary works, *Cooking in Wyoming,* sets forth two very similar recipes, both billed as working for elk or moose. The only difference is in the choice of sweet or sour cream and in sour or sweet milk. I usually use sour cream, or buttermilk, because it is readily available in supermarkets these days. The steaks can be from the loin or hind leg. The latter will be a little tough, or maybe more than a little, in which case they can be simmered longer than the recommended total of 60 minutes, adding water from time to time as needed.

2 pounds elk or moose steaks   **2 tablespoons butter**
2 cups chopped mushrooms   **2 tablespoons flour**
½ medium to large onion,   **½ cup sour cream**
  chopped   **water**

Heat the butter in a skillet. Sauté the onion for a couple of minutes. Sear the steaks on both sides, right over the onion. Add a little water, to about ½ inch, cover, and simmer for 30 minutes. Add the mushrooms. Make a paste of the cream and flour. Stir the paste into the skillet, turning the steaks in the process. Add a little water. Cover and simmer for 30 minutes, or until tender, adding a little water and turning the steaks from time to time.

VENISON ST. HUBERT

Here's a highly marinated venison steak. It's very good, provided that you start with good meat. Marinades really can't help meat that hasn't been properly handled after the kill.

THE STEAKS
2 pounds venison steaks, ¾ inch thick
olive oil

THE MARINADE

2 cups white wine	**2 carrots, chopped**
1 cup white vinegar	**2 cloves garlic, chopped**
½ cup olive oil	**2 bay leaves**
2 medium to large onions,	**1 teaspoon black pepper**
**　sliced**	**1 teaspoon chopped fresh thyme**
2 shallots, chopped	**⅛ teaspoon ground cloves**

THE SAUCE

1 cup brown sauce or	**2 tablespoons red currant jelly**
**　canned beef gravy**	**10 peppercorns, crushed or**
½ cup vinegar	**　coarsely ground**

Place the steaks in a nonmetallic container. Mix the marinade ingredients, pour over the steaks, and place the container in the refrigerator for 24 hours, turning the steaks a time or two. When you are ready to cook, start a sauce by simmering the black pepper and vinegar until it is reduced by half. Add the brown sauce or gravy and simmer very slowly for 30 minutes. Stir in the jelly. Strain and keep warm until the steaks are ready. Heat the olive oil in a cast-iron skillet and cook the steaks for a few minutes on either side, until medium rare. Place the steaks on heated plates or a platter. Top with the sauce. Serve hot.

BORNEAN CHOPS

Here's a culinary treat that I found in (and adapted from) Richard Sterling's book *Dining with Headhunters*. Sterling in turn got it from a native of the jungle called Eetwat, who foraged and processed wild pepper. Wild pigs, I understand, abound in the jungles of Borneo, feeding on native fruits. Highly prized as table fare, they are hunted by the rather nomadic Punan peoples with poisoned dart and blowgun. Anyhow, I tried Eetwat's recipe with loin chops from a Florida pineywood rooter, with the white pepper from a local supermarket (bottled in brine), with the juice of two large Parson Brown oranges (a variety developed on Timucuan Island in Lake Weir, where I once lived), with peanut oil from the Wiregrass area of Alabama, where I was raised on a peanut farm, and with wild onions that grow profusely along the roadways of North America and in my backyard. Use chops from domestic pig if you must, cutting them about 1 inch thick, and try scallions with green tops in lieu of wild onions. Or ramps, in season.

2 pounds loin chops	¼ cup peanut oil
juice of 2 oranges	2 cups flour
¼ cup sliced scallions or wild onions with part of tops	2 tablespoons salt
	2 tablespoons black pepper
¼ cup green peppercorns	

Mix the flour, salt, and black pepper in a brown bag. Shake the chops to coat all sides. Heat the peanut oil in a large cast-iron skillet. Brown on both sides, cooking in two or more batches if necessary. Remove the chops, putting them on a brown bag to drain. Sauté the scallions for 5 or 6 minutes. Place the chops back into the skillet, add the orange juice, cover, and simmer until the chops are almost done. Remove the chops, add the green peppercorns, and reduce the pan liquid until you have a nice sauce. Pour the sauce over the chops, let sit for a minute or two, and serve with rice and steamed vegetables of your choice.

PORK LOIN STEAKS

It's hard to go wrong with pork chops—except for overcooking by dry heat. These can be cut and cooked with the bone in, T-bone- or porterhouse-style, or the loin muscles can be removed from the backbone and sliced separately. (What's left makes wonderful soup.) I prefer the T-bone style for broiling or grilling, but for this recipe, cooked in a skillet, I find that boned chops are easier to fit into the available space. Even so, you will need a large skillet with a cover for this recipe. The dish is from South America, where the recipe can be used with Venezuelan capybara and piglike rooters of the Amazon basin. If you are working with European boar, wild pig, or warthog, you might want to marinate the chops overnight in a mixture of 1 tablespoon of baking soda dissolved in a quart of water (or consider the marinades in chapter 12).

2 pounds pork loin steaks, ½ inch thick	**2 tablespoons lard or bacon drippings**
juice of 1 lemon	**½ cup white vinegar**
	salt and pepper to taste

Pat the pork steaks dry with a paper towel and sprinkle on both sides with lemon juice. It's best to sprinkle the steaks one at a time, then stack them atop each other. Let these stand for 1 hour. Heat the lard or bacon drippings in the skillet to medium-high heat. Brown the steaks on each side. Sprinkle the steaks with salt and pepper, then add the vinegar. Cover the skillet, reduce the heat to low, and simmer for 30 or 40 minutes, turning from time to time, or until the meat is very tender.

SKILLET EMU, RHEA, OR OSTRICH STEAKS

These big birds produce a delicious red meat and can be cooked in a skillet just like beefsteaks. Here's a recipe that I recommend for a skilletful of either ostrich, emu, or the smaller rhea. See chapter 10 for more information about these big, flightless birds, designed for running wild on the planes of Africa (ostrich), Australia (emu), and South America (rhea). These birds are raised on farms these days (in America and abroad) and the meat is available commercially.

2 pounds steak, about
  1½ inches thick
8 ounces fresh mushrooms
½ cup chopped green onions
  with part of tops
½ cup whipping cream
¼ cup bourbon

¼ cup butter (divided)
3 tablespoons prepared mustard
1 tablespoon honey
flour
salt and freshly ground
  black pepper

Melt 2 tablespoons of butter in a large, heavy skillet. Sauté the green onions and mushrooms for about 5 minutes. Remove with a slotted spoon, draining them as you go, and set aside. Melt the rest of the butter in the skillet. Salt and pepper the steaks, dust lightly in flour, and cook for 5 minutes on each side, more or less, depending on the thickness. For best results, the steaks should be medium rare. Remove the steaks to heated plates or a serving platter. Quickly put the mushrooms and green onions back into the skillet. Add the bourbon, mustard, honey, and cream. Simmer—but do not boil—until the sauce thickens. Pour the sauce over the steaks and send to the table immediately.

Steaks under the Broiler

3

*With all of man's genius for putting to his own use the good things
of the earth, with all his imagination and artistry, he has never discovered
any edible which excels good roast beef or a good broiled steak.*
—Brigadier General Frank Dorn

Broiling a steak under the source of heat, a relatively modern
way of cooking as compared with grilling over the heat, is usually
accomplished in the oven of an electric or gas stove. Electric ovens
work best, partly because they have both top and bottom heating elements. Gas ovens usually have only one burner, at the bottom. Often
this arrangement puts the broiling pan only a few inches off the floor,
and, personally, I don't like to get on my knees to cook steaks.

For the best gustatory results, the top of the steaks should be
from 3 to 4 inches from the heat. (I'll even go up to 2 inches, if somebody else has to clean the oven.) This arrangement can sometimes be
achieved by putting the broiling rack in the top slot, but sometimes
a broiling pan must be used atop a shallow baking pan, inserted
upside down as a filler. Taking the trouble to get the right distance is
worth the effort, letting you broil a steak that is almost crusty on the
outside, moist and juicy and rosy in the middle. Be warned, howev-

er, that putting the meat so close to the heat causes the fat to spatter onto the oven walls, making a mess. I don't worry about this, but it helps to have the steaks on a rack well above the drip pan.

Also, remember to leave the oven door open while broiling steaks, if you are using an electric oven with the heating elements on top. Closing the door causes the meat to bake as well as broil.

As a rule, steaks should be broiled 4 or 5 minutes on each side, without a lot of turning, allowing a minute or two either way, depending on the thickness of the meat, the intensity of heat, and the distance between the top of the meat and the heat. Do not overcook. I recommend using a timer to remind yourself to turn or check the steaks, especially if you will busy yourself making salad or setting the table or chatting with the guests while cooking the steaks. The perfectionist may prefer to cook the steaks a little longer on the first side. For a total cooking time of 8 minutes, for example, try 4½ minutes on the first side and 3½ after the turn. And, by the way, always turn the steaks with tongs or perhaps a spatula.

On the whole, broiling is an excellent way to cook steaks. The one complication is that broiling takes up the oven, making it difficult to bake the potatoes and heat the bread while cooking the steak. Small countertop auxiliary broilers can be used for cooking a steak or two, but as a rule these don't get as hot as a good kitchen stove and for that reason don't do a good job of browning the outside surfaces. It's really best to have two regular ovens—one for baking and one for broiling. Lacking that luxury, try baking the potatoes first. They will hold the heat for some time, especially if they are not wrapped in aluminum foil, which conducts away heat.

MAFIA STEAK FLORENTINE WITH MUSHROOMS

This dish, as reported in *The Mafia Cookbook* by Joseph "Joe Dogs" Iannuzzi, was served up at a sort of coming-out party for Tommy Agro, who, "like any other guy fresh from the joint," wanted steak.

Also present at the feast were Iannuzzi himself (who apparently cooked the steaks), Skinny Bobby DeSimone, Louie Esposito, and Buzzy Faldo. Excuse me, boys, for thinking that the term "Florentine" in a recipe denotes spinach, but, hey, I'm not going to argue the point with Joe Dogs Iannuzzi and, frankly, I'm glad to see that he really doesn't want any spinach with steak.

5 New York strip steaks	3 cloves garlic, sliced thinly with
2 pounds mushrooms, sliced	a single-edge razor blade
¼ cup cognac	1 shallot, finely chopped
3 tablespoons chopped	juice of ½ lemon
fresh parsley	3½ tablespoons butter
2 tablespoons chopped	2 teaspoons extra-virgin olive oil
fresh chives	salt and pepper

About 25 minutes before broiling the steaks, heat the butter and olive oil in a large skillet. Add the mushrooms, salt, and pepper. Cook for 10 minutes, stirring and tossing the mushrooms about as you go. Add the parsley, chives, shallot, and garlic. Cook for 7 minutes. Add the cognac and lemon juice. Reduce the heat and simmer for 5 minutes. Preheat the broiler and cook the steaks for about 4 minutes on each side, or until done to your liking. Joe Dogs says that rare is preferred, but I want mine medium rare. When the steaks are ready, place one on each plate and top with mushrooms and pan drippings. Serve with steamed asparagus topped with hollandaise sauce, along with long loaves of crusty Italian bread.

HERTER'S BUTTER KNIFE STEAK

According to George Leonard Herter, coauthor of *Bull Cook and Authentic Historical Recipes and Practices,* this steak is best made with a sirloin 2¼ inches thick—cut into rounds to make it look like filet mignon. In my version, I will allow the use of a thick ribeye or perhaps a chuckeye. Note also that thinner steaks can also be used, adjusting the cooking times and the distance from the heat. One of the juiciest steaks I've ever eaten was cooked in keeping with this method many years ago by a young lady of my desire. I also remember the loaf of French bread, torn off in pieces and used to sop the gravy.

sirloin, 2¼ inches thick
butter
salt and pepper

Preheat the broiler. Adjust the rack to position the top of the steak 4 inches under the heat. Sprinkle a layer of salt in a plate. Dip both sides of the steak into salt, then sprinkle with black pepper. Place the steak in a broiling pan. With the oven door partly open, broil the steak, turning from time to time and basting with butter and pan juice, until done to your liking. (Note that these steaks are 2¼ inches thick, which requires longer cooking times and several turns.) Put the steaks onto plates, smear with butter, and serve immediately. Steaks cooked in this manner, Herter says, can be cut with a butter knife.

STUFFED BROILED STEAKS

This recipe works best with bone-in cuts such as rib or club steaks. A club steak, of course, is similar to a T-bone with very little or no round of tenderloin. The advantage of such a steak is that the slit for holding the stuffing can be made all the way to the bone, which helps hold things together.

4 to 6 club steaks,
    1½ inches thick
8 ounces fresh button
    mushrooms
8 green onions, chopped
    with part of tops

2 cloves garlic, finely chopped
¼ cup butter
½ cup dry red wine
1 tablespoon Worcestershire sauce
salt and freshly ground
    black pepper

In a skillet, sauté the green onions, mushrooms, and garlic in butter for 4 or 5 minutes on medium heat. Add the wine, Worcestershire sauce, salt, and pepper. Simmer for 3 or 4 minutes. Cut large pockets into each steak, going down to the bone. Stuff the mushroom mixture into the steaks. Skewer shut with toothpicks. Preheat the broiler, adjusting the rack to position the surface of the meat about 3 inches from the heat (for steaks 1½ inches thick). Broil for 4 or 5 minutes, then turn and broil for 4 or 5 minutes on the other side, or until medium rare or to your liking. After turning, sprinkle each steak with salt and pepper. Serve hot, along with steamed asparagus, stuffed potato skins, hot bread, and red wine.

DRESSING A SIRLOIN FOR THE GENERAL

In *A General's Diary of Treasured Recipes*, Brigadier General Frank Dorn spoke of eating a memorable steak with friends, served with cheese dressing, a green salad, and hard French rolls. "I could have gorged for hours," he said. Well, I don't know how long it would take the general to eat a 2-pound sirloin, but I cooked one with his recipe and found it to be quite filling, partly because of the heavy cream and Roquefort.

2-pound sirloin steak
3 ounces blue cheese
  or Roquefort
2 tablespoons heavy cream

2 tablespoons freshly grated
  horseradish
salt and pepper
garlic

Preheat the broiler. Cut a clove or two of garlic in half, then rub both sides of the sirloin. Sprinkle with salt and pepper. Place the steak under the broiler, about 3 inches from the heat, for 5 minutes. While waiting, mash together the cheese, horseradish, and cream. Turn the steak and broil for 3 or 4 minutes, until almost medium rare. Quickly spread the steak with the cheese dressing, place it back under the heat, and cook until the cheese melts and begins to brown. Serve hot, along with plenty of green salad and hard French rolls, perhaps with good red wine.

LONDON BROIL

Although this term is often used these days to denote a special cut of beef (flank steak), it is really a method of cooking and serving a very lean steak. Traditionally it is served with mushroom sauce, although many modern recipes call instead for a marinade or rub with half a dozen spices. The flank steak is a nice, juicy piece of meat, but it contains little marbling and if cooked too long it dries out, becomes chewy, and loses flavor. Carving such a steak is almost as important as cooking it: The steak should be sliced thinly on the bias, after it has been cooked. I prefer to cut the cooked steak into serving-size chunks, letting the diner do the slicing at the table. This method puts most of the natural juice on the plate and preserves the concept of a steak, but for one reason or another many people prefer to slice the meat before serving, possibly because some of their guests may not know how to carve it properly. It helps to have a sharp knife.

1 flank steak, about 2 pounds
olive oil
juice of 1 lemon
1 tablespoon chopped
  fresh parsley
2 cloves garlic, minced

1 teaspoon chopped fresh
  rosemary or marjoram
salt and freshly ground
  black pepper
Hungarian paprika

Sprinkle the steak on both sides with pepper, paprika, and salt. Place it into a suitable dish, then squeeze the lemon juice over it. Sprinkle on the garlic, parsley, and rosemary. Pour in a little olive oil, turning the steak several times to coat all sides. Marinate the steak in the refrigerator for 2 or 3 hours. When you are ready to cook, preheat the broiler and adjust the rack to position the top of the meat 6 inches below the heat source. Cook until rare or medium rare, 6 or 7 minutes on each side. Serve hot with a mushroom sauce. (If you like a strong flavor, try the mushroom ketchup in chapter 12, made from an old English country recipe.)

Note: Other cuts of meat, such as bottom round, chuck steak, or sirloin tip, can be used instead of flank steak. Also see the comments about flank steaks in chapter 9.

BROILED STEAKS JACK UBALDI

It is important, Jack Ubaldi says in his *Meat Book,* to preheat the broiler at least 15 minutes ahead of time. If you don't, he warned, the steak may steam instead of broil, turning out gray meat and a panful of juice instead of a steak with a juicy, pink inside. It's a good point. He allows marinades and spreads or sauces, such as mustard or Worcestershire—but his personal preference is quite simple:

Broil the steak on one side, then sprinkle the cooked side with salt. Broil the other side. Just before serving, add a pat of butter and a little lemon juice to each steak. Serve hot.

HAWAIIAN STEAK

Here's a broiled steak as sometimes cooked in Hawaii, showing Asian influence. Although broiled, the steak makes good use of the meat's natural juices.

The measures below are for one steak. Increase as needed. The marinade, I might add, is not unlike some of the bottled steak seasonings on the market, being composed primarily of soy sauce.

1 filet mignon, cut about 3 inches thick	**1 clove garlic, minced**
	1 inch fresh gingerroot, minced
½ cup soy sauce	**freshly ground black pepper**

Butterfly the filet mignon and put it into a nonmetallic container. Mix the rest of the ingredients and pour over the steak, turning it to coat all sides evenly. Marinate for 4 hours, turning from time to time.

Preheat the broiler and adjust the rack to put the steak about 3 inches from the heat. Place the steak (in butterfly position, dripping with marinade) directly into a broiling pan (without a rack). Broil for 4 minutes, turn and broil for 3 minutes, or until medium rare or done to your liking. Baste a time or two with juices from the pan. Serve on a heated platter, spooning pan juices over it. Tilt the broiling pan in order to get every drop.

STEAK MIRABEAU

This great recipe works best with boneless, tender steaks. Large ribeyes are perfect. This dish makes an attractive presentation on a large platter, for which you can butterfly a 3-inch ribeye steak, then wrap it in two or three strips of bacon, pinned with round toothpicks or small skewers, to hold it together.

ribeye steaks	**stuffed black olives,**
olive oil	**thinly sliced in rounds**
canned anchovy fillets	**freshly ground black pepper**

Preheat the broiler. Warm the steak platters or plates. Brush each steak with olive oil, then sprinkle both sides with black pepper. Broil the steaks close to the heat until cooked medium rare. Put the steaks onto the heated plates or serving platters. Decorate the top of each steak with a 1- by 2-inch diamond lattice of anchovy fillets. Place a slice of olive in the center of each triangle. Serve hot with sautéed mushrooms, steamed asparagus, and several small boiled new potatoes. This makes an attractive dish, especially when made with large, shiny black olives stuffed with red pimento.

Variation: If you like the combined flavor of steak and anchovy, consider basting the steaks lightly with a little Asian fish sauce. This can be mixed in with the olive oil.

A. D.'S T-BONES FOR TWO

The recipe works best with electric heat, but I have also cooked it under a gas flame during my more ardent college days.

2 T-bone or porterhouse steaks
cracked peppercorns
freshly ground sea salt

Sprinkle each steak on both sides with cracked or coarsely ground black peppercorns. Let stand for an hour or so. Preheat the broiler and adjust the rack just right to put the top of the meat 3 inches from the heating coils. Broil the steaks for 4 minutes on each side, or until the surface is nicely browned on the outside and, hopefully, juicy and pink on the inside, turning only once. Sprinkle each steak with salt and send to the table, preferably on a heated plate. Eat hot.

JAMAICAN RUM STEAKS

The current heat wave of recipes calling for incineratory marinades and jerk rubs, usually made with those island Scotch bonnet peppers, has given Jamaican cookery a bad name among those who like to stay on the lower end of the Scoville scale. For a change, here's a Jamaican recipe without any chili at all.

ribeyes
rum butter (see chapter 12 for recipe)
salt and black pepper

Salt and pepper the steaks to taste. Broil the steaks about 3 inches under the heat source until medium rare, usually about 4 minutes on each side. Place the steaks on heated serving plates and put a pat or two of rum butter on each one. Serve hot with cooked (very ripe) plantains, chayote, yard-long beans, or other island vegetables. If you prefer, use baked potatoes or even spinach. But be sure to follow the feast with green mango fool. (See the recipe in chapter 11.)

JUDY MARSH'S BEAR STEAK SICILIANO

Bear is hard to come by these days, but some states do offer hunting seasons, and sometimes the meat is available by mail order or in outlets that traffic in venison and game meat. In any case, I adapted this recipe from *The Maine Way,* a collection of recipes for fish and game. If bear isn't readily available, use any good cut of meat. Loin steaks are especially good. The recipe calls for a meat tenderizer, which I don't normally use; but it works and can make good eating from very tough steaks. A good cut of prime bear really doesn't need a tenderizer. As with other kinds of game—as well as beef and pork—the animal should be killed quickly and promptly field-dressed. A bear (or a deer) that has been chased with dogs may not be fit to eat, in which case no amount of tenderizer or marinade will help very much.

3 or 4 pounds bear steaks, 1½ inches thick	**2 tablespoons butter**
meat tenderizer	**2 tablespoons prepared mustard**
1 cup burgundy	**1 tablespoon Worcestershire sauce**
1 small to medium onion, minced	**1 tablespoon sugar**
1 clove garlic, minced	**1 teaspoon salt**
	¼ teaspoon pepper
	¼ teaspoon dried oregano

Sprinkle the steaks on both sides with meat tenderizer, piercing the surface of the meat here and there with a fork. Melt the butter in a pot and mix in the rest of the ingredients. Let the marinade cool, then pour it over the steaks in a nonmetallic container. Marinate in the refrigerator for several hours, turning a time or two. Preheat the broiler. Put the steaks into a broiling pan. In a saucepan, bring the marinade to a boil, then remove from the heat. Baste the steaks on both sides with the marinade and broil 4 inches from the heat source for 5 minutes on each side, or until medium rare. Baste again and broil for another minute. Remove the steaks to a serving platter. Pour the drippings from the broiling pan into the basting sauce (marinade) and reduce to a gravy to be served with the steaks. Serve hot, along with steamed vegetables, bread, and the rest of the burgundy.

BROILED LAMB SADDLE STEAKS

Lamb provides excellent T-bones, cut from a split loin. If the loin is left whole (unsplit), the two T-bones are left intact. I call these saddle steaks, but they are sometimes called English chops. For best results when broiling, they should be about 1½ inches thick. I marinate the steaks, usually with the aid of lemon juice or perhaps onion juice and garlic. For serving, allow at least two T-bones for each diner, or one English chop. Note that lamb or mutton are best when broiled a little slower than beef. For this reason, the rack is a little farther from the heat source.

4 saddle steaks (or 8 lamb T-bones)	1 teaspoon chopped fresh thyme
juice of 2 lemons	olive oil
3 cloves garlic, minced	salt and freshly ground black pepper

Place the chops into a large nonmetallic container or zip-bag. Mix the lemon juice, garlic, thyme, and a little black pepper and sprinkle it evenly over the chops. Turn the chops with your hands to coat all surfaces. Marinate for 1 hour or longer in the refrigerator. Preheat the broiler, positioning the rack about 5 inches from the heat source. Drain the chops and brush each side with olive oil. Broil for 5 minutes, turn and broil for 4 minutes, or until the chop is cooked medium rare—golden brown on the surface but still pink inside. Sprinkle each chop lightly with salt. Serve hot, along with mint jelly or mint sauce and perhaps a few springs of green mint for garnish, if readily available.

Note: Rib chops can be used instead of saddle cuts. Have them cut two ribs per chop, making them thick and juicy.

STEAKS IN THE OVEN

4

ALTHOUGH STEAKS CAN be baked successfully, the method really doesn't fit nicely into the spirit of this book. I prefer hands-on cooking, such as grilling outdoors with tongs in one hand and a beer in the other, or skillet shaking on the kitchen stovetop, instead of shutting the steaks up inside an oven. (Even when broiling, if done properly with the oven door open, one can watch and smell the steaks being cooked.) Still, steaks cooked slowly in the oven can be very tasty, especially if gravy is made from the pan drippings. Boneless chuck steaks are especially tasty when cooked by this method.

Many of the better baked recipes call for rolling the steaks, or stuffing them in one way or another. I've seen a recipe for rolled flank steak calling for ground veal, ground pork, bacon, sliced salami, and several cheeses, along with a dozen other ingredients. Good, maybe; even excellent, perhaps. But it's simply not a steak. I feel the same way about beef Wellington. It's a roast, not a steak.

Moreover, baking the steaks usually requires an hour or more and conflicts with cooking the potatoes and heating the bread, unless you've got two ovens.

EASY BAKED STEAK

Here's a simple recipe that works with round or chuck steaks, and can, of course, be used with better cuts. You'll need a covered baking pan large enough to contain the steaks without overlapping.

2 pounds steaks, ½ inch thick　　　**1 cup flour**

1 cup butter, melted　　　**salt and pepper**

Preheat the oven to 350 degrees. Cut the steaks into serving-size pieces. Sprinkle both sides with salt and pepper and fit nicely into the baking pan. Mix the flour into the butter, then spread the mixture over the tops of the steaks. Cover the pan and bake in the center of the oven for 40 minutes. Do not turn. Remove the lid and cook for an additional 20 minutes. Serve hot.

URUGUAYAN ROUND STEAK

South America raises lots of cattle, especially in Argentina. According to *The South American Cook Book* (written some time ago by Cora, Rose, and Bob Brown, to whom I am indebted for this recipe and much good information), Uruguay produces some excellent beef. Many of the authentic recipes are for cooking either stew meat or large chunks of meat. The steaks are often cooked in the oven, as in this recipe. It calls for beef suet. Substitute vegetable oil if you must.

2½ pounds round steaks　　　**1 clove garlic**

1 cup beef broth　　　**1 teaspoon chili powder**

2 ounces beef suet (beef fat)　　　**¼ teaspoon cayenne**

4 medium to large onions　　　**flour**

2 medium to large tomatoes,　　　**salt and pepper**
**　sliced**

Preheat the oven to 350 degrees. Fry the suet in a skillet until all the oil cooks out. Slice one of the onions and sauté in the fat, along with the garlic and chili power. Remove the onions and garlic, saving them for the gravy. Salt the steaks on both sides, sprinkle with cayenne, and dust with flour. Then brown the steaks in the remaining beef suet in the skillet. Place the steaks in a baking pan. Slice the rest of the onions and place over the steaks. Put the pan into the oven and bake for about 40 minutes. Place the tomato slices on top. Sprinkle with salt and pepper. Bake for 30 to 40 minutes, until the steak is very tender. While waiting, make a gravy in the skillet, using the beef broth, a little flour, and the reserved onions; keep warm. When the steaks are done, remove them to a serving platter. Pour the gravy into the baking pan, mix with the juices, bring to a boil, and spoon over the steaks. Serve hot, along with mashed potatoes or rice and vegetables.

Note: Another dish, cariucho, is also cooked in Ecuador. Salt and pepper 2 pounds of flank steaks. Bake in the oven, preheated to 350 degrees. Cover with slices of boiled potatoes. Over all this pour a cariucho sauce, made as follows: Heat 2 tablespoons of lard in a skillet. Sauté 2 minced onions and 1 minced green pepper for 5 minutes. Add two large tomatoes, peeled and sliced. Cook until the sauce is bubbly. Add 1 pint scalded milk and ¼ cup peanut butter. Simmer, stirring as you go, until the sauce is smooth and thick. Pour over the steaks, garnishing with minced parsley and chopped hard-boiled eggs.

BAKED HAM STEAK

It's hard to go wrong with modern precooked "cured" hams as sold in supermarkets, most of which are pumped up with water and perhaps curing agents. A long, slow baking cooks out most of the water. For a 2-inch ham, try an hour at 300 degrees. Then baste the ham with a honey-mustard sauce, into which has been mixed a little freshly ground black pepper, and broil it under intense heat until it browns nicely. Serve it hot along with mashed potatoes and ham gravy, fresh vegetables, and hot biscuits.

A fully cured country ham steak is too dry and salty for this recipe. If you use one, it's best to soak it overnight in several changes of water. Then bake it.

CROSS CREEK BAKED HAM STEAK

For this recipe, I am head over heels in debt to Marjorie Kinnan Rawlings, author of *The Yearling* and *Cross Creek Cookery,* a book that has been in print since 1942. Mrs. Rawlings cooked with an old iron stove (which I have seen; and I remember my mother cooking on one years ago) and a cast-iron skillet. Some modern skillets have handles that will burn in the oven. If you are using a fully salt-cured ham, be sure to freshen it overnight in several changes of water.

center-cut ham steak with some fat around it	flour
milk	boiling water
	salt and pepper

Preheat the oven to 300 degrees. Place the ham steak into a skillet. Cover it with milk, along with a little salt and pepper. (A fully cured ham will need no salt.) Place the skillet in the center of the oven and cook until a skin forms on the top of the milk. Stir this into the meat. Repeat until the liquid has evaporated, leaving only the residue and the fat that has cooked out of the meat. If the ham is not tender at this point, add a little boiling water and continue to cook until the ham is ready, turning and adding more water all along as needed. When it is very tender, remove the ham to a serving platter and keep it warm. Drain most of the fat out of the skillet, leaving about 2 tablespoons of it. Place the skillet on the stove burner (or eye if you are using a woodstove) and stir in 1½ tablespoons of flour. Slowly add 1 cup of milk. Simmer for 2 minutes, stirring all the while. Pour some of the gravy over the ham and serve the rest separately in a bowl.

Mrs. Rawlings liked to serve this ham with baked sweet potatoes and cornmeal muffins, followed by brown Betty for dessert. This is Big Scrub eating at its uncomplicated best.

VEAL LAUSANNE

Here's a recipe that works with veal cutlets or steaks, preferably tender cuts from the loin area. Each cutlet should be about 1 inch thick.

2 pounds veal cutlets	**8 ounces fresh mushrooms, sliced**
⅓ cup light cream	**1 medium to large onion, cut into rings**
¼ cup red or white wine	**flour**
¼ cup olive oil	**salt and pepper**

Preheat the oven to 375 degrees. Sprinkle the cutlets with salt and pepper, then dust with flour, coating both sides. Heat the oil in a skillet and quickly brown the cutlets two or three at a time. As you go, arrange the cutlets in a shallow, greased baking dish. Sauté the onions and arrange them over the meat, along with the sliced mushrooms. Pour in the cream and wine, distributing both equally over the surface. Place the pan in the center of the oven. Bake for 40 minutes, or until nicely tender.

Easy Variation: Use a can of condensed mushroom soup instead of fresh mushrooms and cream.

BRANDING-IRON AND GRILLING MACHINE STEAKS

5

CAST-IRON SKILLETS and griddles have been cooking superior steaks for decades, and cast iron, if properly seasoned and correctly used, is the original nonstick cooking surface. In order to maintain the nonstick quality, however, cast-iron pieces are cleaned with only a wet sponge or paper towel, or perhaps by washing them lightly with mild soap and warm water. Keeping cast iron at cooking readiness requires lots of tender loving care, and, as I pointed out in my book *Cast-Iron Cooking,* the worst thing you can do to a well-seasoned skillet is to scrub it with some abrasive or steam it in a modern dishwasher.

The best cast-iron skillets or griddles have a very smooth cooking surface. In recent years, however, some manufacturers, apparently in an attempt to cut production costs, have started marketing some of their skillets with a rough cooking surface. These are harder to clean and use.

The new raised-rib skillets and griddles are even harder to clean. Yet, they are seen everywhere in our stores and mail-order catalogs these days, and many of them are no doubt wrapped in red and put under the Christmas tree. I can't recall, however, ever seeing anybody actually cook with one, either in the kitchen, on the patio, in camp, or on a TV show. The two-burner rectangular raised-rib griddles are even harder than skillets to clean simply because of their large size and cast-iron weight.

The raised rib is a very salable idea, however. With it one can cook a steak or a burger with parallel char marks, which resemble steaks cooked on a grill. These no doubt add to the visual appeal of the finished steak. In *Bull Cook and Authentic Historical Recipes,* George Leonard Herter said that some restaurants make these marks with an iron poker heated on hot coals. This is really not a bad idea, and at one time such an iron poker, called a salamander, was used as a cooking aid.

While most modern cooks agree that the marks add an appealing visual touch to the steak, the higher purpose of the raised-rib design is to drain the fat away from the meat. It will do that, to a degree. But it also drains away some tasty steak juice, which is, I might add, the very essence of skillet cookery. The raised ribs make it almost impossible to stir up a sauce or gravy in the skillet, using the tasty dredgings scraped up from the bottom of the pan. In short, the raised ribs preclude such classic recipes as steak Diana—or even a good country steak smothered in its own gravy.

And the worst is yet to come. After cooking, you've got all that crap between the ribs of the skillet or griddle. When cooking on a grill, by comparison, most of the stuff falls between the cracks and burns.

Of course, some rather expensive raised-rib skillets and griddles are coated with Teflon, ceramic glaze, or some such nonstick surface. In my experience, these coatings don't last for high-heat skillet cooking, either wearing away, peeling off, or cracking. But they are no doubt getting better, and I don't rule out using one in the future. For raised-rib cooking, slick Teflon pieces might well be more practical than cast-iron simply because they permit a little more scrubbing or easier cleaning.

I don't have a recipe for raised-rib cooking, but it's a very easy way to go. Simply heat the skillet or griddle until it is quite hot, lay on a steak, cook for 4 minutes, turn, baste, and cook the other side until the steak is medium rare. Turn only once, and do not move the steak about, if you want distinct char marks. Season to taste with salt and pepper, and serve hot. Easy—until you get to the cleanup.

Clearly, I am not overly enthusiastic about the raised-rib skillets or griddles. The new George Foreman Grilling Machines, on the other hand, do a quick job and work pretty much (but not quite) as billed. These cook by heating simultaneously from the top and bottom, exactly like a waffle iron. The design features a floating hinge, allowing one to cook either thick or thin steaks (but not at the same time).

The Grilling Machine cooks twice as fast as a regular grill. With mine I can cook a buffalo ribeye 1½ inches thick in 4 minutes, sharp, for medium rare, give or take a second or two. A timer helps the cook zero in. My Grilling Machine is the medium size, but the larger model is sorely needed and would be most welcome at my house at Yuletide. Also, there are similar machines imported from Italy and France. One of these features removable grilling plates, allowing one to switch from branding iron to smooth griddle to Belgian waffle. Another model folds out flat, thereby doubling your cooking surface, if so desired. This model also has a thermostat, allowing you to adjust the temperature. (The Foreman design is either on or off, as indicated by a red light.) In the future, we will no doubt see other variations on this theme simply because cooking with them is so easy.

The Grilling Machine doesn't get quite hot enough to suit me, but this is the price one must pay for a modern nonstick surface. I would prefer to brand the steaks with cast iron on very high heat, reducing the cooking time even farther.

The Grilling Machine slopes to the front, permitting the fat and good juices to drain down to a handy drip pan. The slope also causes the meat to slide down, or tend to do so. I have even had hot dogs and sausages jump the rail when I opened the top, splashing into the drip pan or, worse, falling onto the floor. I don't want to rile George Foreman here but I'll also have to say, in all honesty, that the Grilling Machine doesn't knock out *all* the fat, as implied or said in advertisements. I hold that well-marbled ribeyes will retain most of their interior fat simply because these things cook in only 4 minutes or so. There's simply not enough time to cook out the fat, draining from top to bottom. If you want really low-fat steaks, it's best to cook with a well-trimmed, scantily marbled flank steak.

The drip feature and slick surface do, however, make the machine easier to clean, bearing in mind that it, being electrical, can't be immersed in water. Foreman recommends cleaning it partly with a grooved plastic spatula provided with the machine, then merely wiping the ribbed surface off with a damp sponge. This seems to work pretty well for me, but modern salmonella-fearing cooks who wash everything with Lysol or Clorox will probably be left with a nagging feeling that the machine needs rinsing.

In any case, here are a few recipes to try on your Grilling Machine.

GRILLING MACHINE NEW YORK STRIPS

I use this recipe when I'm in a hurry. It calls for Dale's Steak Seasoning, which doesn't require a long marinating time. If I'm really in a hurry, I'll microwave a couple of large potatoes instead of heating up the oven. I'll even allow a package of premixed salad from the supermarket, and a loaf of bakery bread. The recipe works best with steaks about 1 inch thick. Avoid thick T-bones or porterhouses, but try ribeyes or even chuckeye steaks as well as the New York strips recommended in the ingredients list.

2 New York strip steaks, 1 inch thick
Dale's Steak Seasoning
freshly ground pepper

Grind some pepper onto both sides of the steaks, setting the mill on coarse. Put the peppered steaks into a nonmetallic container and pour on a little Dale's Steak Seasoning. Turn to coat the steaks on all sides. Marinate for about 10 minutes, or a little longer, while you set the table and get the salad ready and put the potatoes into the microwave. Plug in the grilling machine. When the red light goes off (indicating that the temperature has maxed out), place the steaks side by side and close the lid. Cook for 4 minutes, or until medium rare. Place the steaks directly on heated plates and serve immediately, along with baked potatoes, salad, bread, and butter. Also have a salt mill loaded with sea salt, along with a pepper mill. The Dale's seasoning contains quite a bit of salt (thanks to the soy sauce), but much depends on how long the steaks are marinated.

SNOOK STEAKS

The rule of thumb has it that fish should be cooked 10 minutes per inch of thickness. With a Grilling Machine, however, the time goes down to 5 minutes per inch, simply because the machine works on both sides at once. What's more, the steaks are juicy and have a nice branding-iron pattern on either side. Snook make nice steaks, but any good mild fish of steaking size will work. Try salmon or large catfish. For best results, the steaks (cut crosswise) should be of uniform thickness, about 1 inch. Fillets don't work quite as well since they aren't of uniform thickness. To get a little juice for this recipe, place a handful of pomegranate seeds in a sieve and press with a pestle or the back of a spoon. The fruits are sometimes available in our supermarkets, and some of us are lucky enough to have pomegranate trees in our garden. If unavailable, however, substitute lemon juice.

2 pounds snook steaks
⅓ cup melted butter
⅓ cup tart pomegranate
  juice or lemon juice

salt and black pepper
pomegranate seeds or
  lemon quarters

Brush the steaks heavily on both sides with a mixture of melted butter and pomegranate or lemon juice. Plug in the Grilling Machine.

When the red light goes off, load the steaks into the machine. Sprinkle lightly with salt and pepper. Close the lid, set the timer for 4 minutes, and toss a salad. When the timer sounds off, brush the steaks heavily with the butter mixture and sprinkle with salt and pepper. Close the lid for another 1 minute, or until done. Do not overcook. Serve hot, along with the salad, quinoa (or rice) pilaf, and a crusty bread. Garnish with pomegranate seeds or lemon quarters, or both.

HAMBURGER STEAKS

The chapter called Steak Burgers covers this topic in some detail, and some of the better recipes depend on a gravy made in the skillet in which the meat was cooked. I am including this recipe here, however, because some people really want to get rid of the fat while retaining the juices, as advertised. I'm not going to belabor the point again, but the plain truth is that the Grilling Machine will indeed serve up a juicy burger in short order. (How much is juice and how much is fat, however, is the question that remains in my mind; somehow, knocking out all the fat while retaining all the juice is a little too good to be true.) In any case, exact timing is the key to succulence. Moreover, the steak burger doesn't have to be turned during the cooking, making it less likely to break apart. This negates the need for mixing chicken egg, flour, and other binders or fillers with the meat.

1 pound ground beef
oyster sauce
salt and pepper

Plug in the machine. After sprinkling the ground beef with salt and freshly ground black pepper, shape it into a steak about 1½ inches thick—but resist the temptation to pat it down firmly. When the red light goes out, carefully place the steak burger onto the heated grill, using a large spatula. Lower the top and cook for 5 minutes. Before removing the steak from the grill, cut into it to see if it is done to your liking. I insist on medium rare: nicely pink with lots of good juice. Place the steak directly on the plate, swab it generously with oyster sauce, and serve with mashed potatoes and English peas. Three cheers for George Foreman.

Campfire and Hearthside Steaks 6

I'M NOT GOING into the mechanics of building a fire in this book, and I'll skip the glowing poetry associated with a good campfire. As for cooking, any of the recipes in the chapter about skillet steaks can be cooked over a campfire—but controlling the heat is a little tricky. There are several schemes for resting the skillet on some sort of rack above hot coals, or you can rake out a small bed of coals and place the skillet directly on them. It's best to have a pair of heavy-duty cooking gloves. These will enable you to remove the skillet from the fire if things get too hot and start to burn. Make sure that you have a sturdy place to set the hot skillet. A swing-away grill is also helpful, and several of these are on the market.

Cooking over an open fire or wood coals can be great fun, but it usually requires lots of squatting, making it a young man's passion. Each young devotee will have his own techniques and bag of tricks. For the older generations, however, I would like to suggest a raised-platform scheme for the fire or at least for hot coals. Such a platform can be built in camp with green saplings, or a more permanent structure can be made in the backyard, using brick, blocks, or wood. One of my favorites was converted from an old but very sturdy outdoor table constructed with pressure-treated lumber. I built a 6-inch frame on top of the table, creating, in effect, a raised sandbox to hold the coals, and reinforced the legs. It worked beautifully. Of course, the sand prevented the coals from burning the top of the table.

Either in camp or at the hearthside, it's almost always best to cook on a small bed of coals piled away from the main fire. A shovel of some sort comes in handy. Before transferring the coals (or before building a fire if you are cooking between two logs or rocks), make sure that your grill or skillet rest is steady and safe. I like a swing-away adjustable grill, either for direct grilling or for holding the skillet. A good pair of no-slip tongs is also good to have so that you can remove the steak from the rack if need be. Heavy-duty cooking gloves can also be used to turn the steaks, but don't use forks unless you want to lose some good juice. In general, remember that wood coals get much hotter than the typical patio grill fueled by charcoal, briquettes, gas, or electric coils.

No matter how you rig for grilling or skillet cooking, be careful with open fires. When you break camp, be sure to wet the area down thoroughly with water or at least cover up the hot coals with dirt.

Usually, for camp cookery, it's best to use simple recipes with a short ingredients list, although some camps do have a rather complete grub box. Here are a few recipes that I consider especially suited for camp and hearthside cooking. Somewhat surprisingly, some of these require no cooking utensils or grills.

CAMP SKILLET STEAKS

Here's a recipe that can be used in camp whenever you have a skillet but no staples like cooking oil or flour. All you need is some salt. A little pepper helps. Any kind of steak or chop can be used, but I like venison loin or butterflied tenderloin. The technique works best with a steak or chop about ¾ inch thick. Be warned that this meat is eatable only if it is cooked rare or medium rare.

steaks
salt
pepper (if available)

Pepper the steaks on both sides and set aside for an hour or so. Heat a cast-iron skillet or griddle until it's hot enough to sizzle a drop of water. Sprinkle the skillet liberally with salt, spreading it evenly to cover all the bottom. Place a steak into the skillet, directly over the salt. Cook for 3 minutes. Turn and cook the other side for 2 or 3 minutes. Serve hot, brushing off any excess salt.

This steak is surprisingly good if it is not cooked too long, but a modern edition of a very old American cookbook advises the reader to wash the cooked steak with water before serving it. Don't do so. If you or your guests fear salt, it's best to avoid the recipe altogether.

BACKLOG STEAKS

Cooking a steak directly on a hot charred log may be in the "believe it or not" category, and may explain the incorrect procedure set forth in a modern version of a classic American cookbook (the same one that recommends washing the steaks in the recipe above). The authors of this culinary tome say to lay a log directly on the fire and place the steak on top. The flames burning on either side of the log, they say, will cook the steak. Well, that's not the way to go, and I don't see how their method can possibly work unless you want a steak that is burnt around the edges and completely raw in the middle.

The correct way is to leave the log on the coals for a long time, until the bottom starts to burn and and char. Then you roll the log over, exposing the charred side, and lay the steak directly on it. Cooking will take only a minute or two on each side, depending on the thickness of the steak. I like to turn the steak (using tongs) every 30 seconds or so, testing for doneness on each turn. When the steak is done, lightly brush off any ash, sprinkle with salt and pepper, and serve hot. Don't worry about a little ash being left on the meat. Many peoples, including the American Indians, especially in the Southwest, add ashes to their cornbread and other foods.

Anyhow, you can try this at home if you have a fireplace or a suit-able place outside to build a fire. Simply put a segment of round log in the back (called a backlog) and build a good roaring fire. When the fire burns down to coals, use your poker (preferably one with a spur) and roll the backlog forward, leaving the glowing side up. Then cook the steak directly on the glowing log. All the smoke will go up the chim-ney—unless you have pulled the log out too far on the hearth.

Before cooking the steak, however, you might as well bury a few potatoes (or even sweet potatoes) in hot ashes for 30 minutes or so. These are delicious, especially if you like rather hard potato skins. You can wrap the potatoes in foil, or perhaps in wet newspaper, if you want them steamed. Corn pone can also be cooked in ashes, either covered in wet or green corn shucks or placed directly on the coals and then covered with ashes. Such bread is sometimes called ash cake.

If you don't have a suitable log, you can cook the steak directly on a bed of hot coals, turning it every 20 seconds or so. Brush off the ashes and serve. If it isn't burnt too badly, this steak will be juicy and tasty, with a nice char on the outside.

BLACKENED BEEF

I include this recipe here because it is best cooked with the aid of hot wood coals from a campfire. And, in spite of a somewhat lengthy ingredients list, it's really not a bad choice for camp cooking if the seasonings are mixed at home and carried along to camp in a small container. Also remember that several ready-mixed blackening seasonings (I call them Cajun dust) are available these days in super-markets and specialty stores; if you use one of these, buy one formu-lated for beef instead of redfish.

Note that some small portable grills don't get the skillet or grid-dle hot enough. Moreover, a cast-iron skillet or griddle is the only good choice for blackening steaks or fish fillets.

The text here has been adapted from my book *Cast-Iron Cook-ing,* which in turn credited the information and recipe to an article in a special 80s issue of *Life* magazine.

The success of the recipe depends in large part, I think, on the seasoned gravy, which is made separately. To make the dish, I use a skillet for the gravy and a griddle for the blackened beef.

THE SEASONINGS

1 tablespoon salt	2½ teaspoons cayenne pepper
1 tablespoon and ¾ teaspoon	2½ teaspoons dry mustard
black pepper	5 teaspoons fennel seeds

Crush the fennel seeds and mix all ingredients. This seasoning will be used in both the gravy and on the meat. I prepare the gravy first so that it will be ready when the meat is blackened.

THE GRAVY

1½ teaspoon blackening	⅔ cup flour
seasonings (from above)	1 cup chopped green onion tops
⅓ cup cooking oil	4 cups beef or chicken stock

Heat the beef or chicken stock in a saucepan and keep it warm. (You can also use plain water or water with bouillon cubes. Also, I have used a diluted ham stock with great success.) In a large skillet, heat the cooking oil and gradually stir in the flour. Cook very slowly for about 5 minutes, stirring constantly, until you have a medium brown roux. Remove the skillet from the heat and stir in the chopped green onion tops. Gradually stir in the warm stock and the seasonings. Put the skillet back on the heat, turn to high, and bring to a boil. Stir, reduce the heat, and simmer uncovered for 15 minutes. Stir once or twice while cooking. During these 15 minutes, get your meat ready to cook so that both meat and gravy will be hot in temperature as well as in seasoning.

THE MEAT

choice beef, preferably	melted butter
tenderloin, ¾ inch thick	seasonings (from above)

Let the meat come to room temperature. Then dip each piece into melted butter. Sprinkle both sides of the meat generously with seasonings, and press some seasonings into the meat with the palm of your hand. Before cooking the meat, it's best to warm individual serving platters in an oven.

Heat a small *ungreased* griddle (preferably oval) on very hot wood coals or on a gas burner. When the griddle is very hot, put one or two pieces of seasoned meat on it. Sizzle for 2 minutes, or until a crust forms on the bottom. Turn the meat with tongs and sizzle the other side for 2 minutes. Using tongs, place the meat onto the serving platter. Spoon on some hot gravy and serve with a good bread, green salad, baked potato—and lots of ice water.

Note: Many cookbooks and magazine articles advise you to brush the griddle or skillet with melted butter or grease of some sort. Don't do it. If the cast iron is hot enough, you'll just get a cloud of smoke. The butter or the oil should go lightly on the surface of the meat. Its purpose is to help pick up and hold a crust of the spice mix.

STEAK BURGERS 7

Don't worry. In this short chapter I'm not getting into hamburger patties, meat loaves, meatballs, and so on that can be made with ground meat. What I have on my mind is a thick, juicy steak-shaped burger, cooked medium rare and served, as often as not, in its own gravy. The best burgers are made from meat ground at home shortly before cooking time. Any good meat grinder will do, and I get by nicely with an old-fashioned hand-cranked sausage mill.

Any good cut of beef can be used for burgers, including round and chuck steaks. Of course, most people with good teeth would not consider making burgers of porterhouse or ribeye. Also, grinding your own meats offers a good opportunity to mix and experiment. My favorite steak burger, for example, is made from 3 parts ground snapping turtle and 1 part pork.

If at all possible, I avoid adding stuff—fillers and binders—to the burger if I've got enough meat to feed everybody. Although wheat flour and chicken egg will help hold the burger together, it's better to use pure meat and proceed carefully.

71

HAMBURGER STEAK WITH ONIONS

Charred onions (sometimes called caramelized) help produce a wonderful gravy for this hamburger steak. A cast-iron skillet is recommended. Ground round steak is my personal favorite, but any good ground beef or ostrich can be used.

2 pounds ground round	**¼ cup chopped fresh parsley**
2 medium onions, thinly sliced	**salt and freshly ground pepper**
1½ cups dry red wine	**olive oil**
¼ cup butter	

Mix a little salt and pepper into the ground meat and shape it into an oval steak about 1½ inches thick. Heat a skillet, add a little olive oil, and cook the steak for 4 or 5 minutes on each side, turning once, or until it is medium rare. Using two spatulas, carefully remove the steak to a heated platter. Add the onions to the skillet. Sauté until the onions are quite brown—almost burned—to bring out the proper flavor. Add the wine. Cook for 4 or 5 minutes, stirring a time or two. Remove the skillet from the heat. Stir in the butter and parsley. Spoon the onions and skillet gravy atop the steak and serve at once, along with mashed potatoes, salad greens, and steamed vegetables.

2-SKILLET STEAK BURGER

I have adapted this recipe from *Stillroom Cookery,* a quaint book by Grace Firth, who called it Mushroom Sauce, saying, "This sauce makes hamburger patties think they are steaks." Advancing the thought a step farther, I make big, juicy steak burgers instead of patties.

THE SAUCE

8 ounces fresh mushrooms, sliced	**1 tablespoon flour**
	1 tablespoon ketchup

¾ **cup white wine**   1 **teaspoon soy sauce**

½ **cup water**   **salt and pepper**

¼ **cup butter**

Melt the butter in skillet #1. Sauté the mushrooms for about 5 minutes. Sprinkle with salt and pepper. Stir in the flour. Add the wine, water, ketchup, and soy sauce. Bring to a light boil, stirring as you go, and set aside. Keep warm.

THE STEAK

2 **pounds ground beef, lean**   **salt and pepper**

blue cheese, crumbled   **cooking oil**

brown sugar

Heat a little oil in skillet #2. Mix some salt and pepper into the ground meat, then shape it into an oblong steak about 1½ to 2 inches thick. Carefully place it into the hot skillet. Cook for about 5 minutes, then turn and sprinkle lightly with brown sugar. Cook for another 5 minutes, then turn again, sprinkle with blue cheese, and simmer until medium rare. Carefully remove the steak to a heated serving platter. Top with the sauce from skillet #1. Serve hot.

HAMBURGER STEAK WITH DRIED MORELS

If you like the flavor of mushrooms, be sure to try this recipe. Cooking dried mushrooms, reconstituted in a little water, intensifies the flavor. Several types of dried mushrooms, including morels, work for this recipe, but avoid the chewy tree fungus kinds, unless you want color and chewy texture instead of flavor. I don't have exact measures for this recipe, but I recommend at least ½ pound of meat and eight dried morels for each person. Remember that the morels will expand as they soak up water. They can be purchased at gourmet food shops and sometimes in supermarkets. The knowledgeable mycologist can usually find plenty of morels or perhaps chanterelles in the wild, and the new kitchen-table dehydrators make it easy to dry them at home.

good burger meat, rather lean	**clarified butter or ghee (chapter 12)**
dried morels	**salt and pepper**
flour	**spring water**

Soak the morels for several hours in some good water. Dry the mushrooms with paper towels. Save the water. Mix the salt and pepper into the burger meat and shape a steak about 1½ inches thick. Heat a little clarified butter in a skillet. Put the steak into the skillet and add the mushrooms around the sides. Cook for 4 or 5 minutes, then turn the steak and mushrooms. Be careful with the steak, lest you break it apart. I use a large spatula on the bottom and another on top to help hold the meat while turning. When the steak is done, pour most of the mushroom water into the skillet and bring to a boil. Using ¼ cup of the water, make a paste with a little flour. When the steak is done, place it on a heated plate. Top with the mushrooms. Pour a little of the flour paste into the skillet, stirring as you go, to make a gravy. Add a little more mushroom water, plain water, or beef stock if needed. Pour the gravy over the steak. Serve hot along with boiled new potatoes, vegetables, hot bread, and good red wine.

Note: I cooked this steak again shortly before sending this book to the publisher, using up my last dried morels. I didn't have quite enough morels, so I added some chopped wild onions, which were growing so profusely on my lawn. Scallions or green onions will do, added with the mushrooms. Be sure to use part of the green onion tops, chopped in ½-inch lengths.

GRILLED (OR BROILED) HAMBURGER STEAKS

You don't really need a recipe for grilling hamburger steaks over coals or gas heat, but you do need a hinged basket. Otherwise you may have trouble turning the steak without it breaking up. Simply mix some lean ground beef, adding salt and pepper to taste, along, perhaps, with a spoon or two of Pickapeppa or oyster sauce. Shape the mixture into a steak about 1½ inches thick. Place the steak in a hinged grilling basket, well greased, and position it 4 or 5 inches above hot coals. Grill for 5 minutes, turn, and grill the other side for 4 minutes, or until done to your liking. If the meat is very fatty, move the basket about on the grill to avoid flame-ups. Serve hot, along with vegetables and perhaps a Creole sauce. If you want the flavor of smoke, add some green or water-soaked wood chips to the coals and cook under a closed hood.

Variations: Try a mixture of 2 parts ground venison and 1 part pork, or ground lamb and beef or ostrich. Note that you can also broil a hamburger steak by the same method. Simply put the hinged basket under the heat and turn after about 5 minutes.

A. D.'S ELKBURGER (OR BEEF) STEAKS

James Beard, the great American culinary sport, put small ice cubes inside hamburger patties in order to keep the meat juicy. It's a good idea—especially with ground game meat, which usually contains very little fat and therefore tends to be dry. But an ice cube has very little flavor, and I suggest that you combine Beard's idea with one from the Australian carpetbagger steak recipes. That is, embed a fresh oyster or two in the meat patty instead of using an ice cube.

The amount of meat specified in this recipe is enough for one large burger steak, just enough to feed one hungry man or two people of normal appetite. If you need more than one steak, cook in two or more batches.

1 pound ground elk
a few small oysters
bacon drippings
2 tablespoons finely diced onion
1 tablespoon minced fresh parsley

hot black coffee
whole-wheat flour or
    sweet acorn meal
salt and freshly ground
    black pepper

Mix the salt and pepper into the ground elk. Shape the mixture into an oval patty about 7 inches long. Then flatten the patty out and add a few oysters in the center. Fold the meat over, covering the oysters, and pat to fuse the two halves into one, making an oval-shaped steak a little larger than a typical ribeye. Heat a little bacon grease in a cast-iron skillet. Add the elk burger, being careful not to break it apart. Cook on medium-high heat for 5 or 6 minutes. Turn very carefully. (I use two spatulas.) While the other side is cooking, sprinkle a little whole-wheat flour on one side of the steak. There should be enough grease in the skillet to moisten the flour; if not, add a little. Stir the flour about with a wooden spoon. Clear a spot and add the minced onions and parsley. Stir the onions about until they soften. If you've timed everything right, the steak should be almost done. Pour a little hot coffee onto the flour and mix in the onions with your wooden spoon. Let the gravy bubble for a minute or so, then spoon some of it over the steak. Move the steak around a little with your spatula, making sure some gravy gets under the bottom. Cover with a lid for a few minutes. Carefully cut into the steak to test for doneness. The meat should be pink but not bloody. If you want the steak well done, add a little more coffee, cover tightly, and cook for a few minutes longer. Cut the steak in half, then carefully place each half directly onto a plate. Spoon a little of the gravy over each steak, saving the rest for the mashed potatoes or rice and possibly some French-cut green beans.

Note: If this steak breaks apart when you are trying to turn it in the skillet, all is not lost. Go ahead and break it up with your wooden spoon, have another drink, stir the works around in the gravy, and serve it up as elk and oyster hash.

STEAKS BY NAME

8

A NUMBER OF RECIPES carry the word "steak," even if they are made with small chunks of meat, as in the British steak and kidney pie. I'm not going to attempt to cover all these dishes, but a few of the recipes may be in order. Here are my favorites.

SWISS STEAK

Round steak about 1½ inches thick works nicely for Swiss steak, but also try rump or chuck steak. These days prepackaged supermarket round steaks aren't but about ¾ inch thick, maybe 1 inch. Ask your butcher to cut you a thicker one. Some recipes omit the tomatoes, but I consider them to be essential. It's best to cook this dish in a pot suitable for cooking both on top of the stove and in the oven. A stovetop cast-iron Dutch oven with a tight-fitting lid is ideal.

2 pounds round steak,
  1½ inches thick

2 cups diced tomatoes

1 cup diced onions

1 cup diced carrots

½ cup diced celery with tops

1 cup beef stock

½ cup dry red wine

½ cup flour

2 tablespoons peanut or
  vegetable oil

1 tablespoon minced garlic

1 tablespoon minced
  fresh parsley

salt and black pepper

Preheat the oven to 300 degrees. Salt and pepper the steak on both sides and cut it into serving-size pieces. Dredge each piece in flour, then beat it with a meat mallet or the edge of a heavy saucer. Turn it, dust with flour, and beat again. Heat the oil in the Dutch oven. A piece or two at a time, sear the steak on both sides, browning it nicely. Pile the browned steak onto a plate and set aside. Reduce the heat to low, then sauté the onion, garlic, celery, and carrots for 5 or 6 minutes. Add the tomatoes and cook for 2 or 3 minutes. Stir in the beef stock, wine, and parsley, along with a little salt and pepper. Add the browned steak pieces back to the Dutch oven, dunking them under the sauce. Cover and cook in the center of the oven for about 2½ hours, until the steak is very tender. Check a time or two, adding a little water if needed. Serve hot with mashed potatoes, spooning some gravy over each serving.

SALISBURY STEAK

These are sometimes cooked as pones or thick patties, but I think a whole "steak" works better.

2 pounds ground lean beef

3 slices white bread, trimmed,
  shredded, and soaked in milk

¼ cup bread crumbs

1 medium onion, minced

3 slices bacon

1 tablespoon Worcestershire sauce

salt and freshly ground
  black pepper

In a skillet, fry the bacon until crisp. Crumble the bacon and set aside. Sauté the onion in the bacon drippings. Preheat the broiler. In a bowl, mix the ground beef and white bread, working in the salt, pepper, and Worcestershire. Shape the mixture into an oval steak and carefully place it onto a broiling rack. Cook 4 inches from the heat for 5 minutes. Meanwhile, mix the bacon, remaining bacon grease, onion, and bread crumbs. Turn the steak carefully. Top with the onion and bacon mixture, spreading it evenly. Broil for about 5 minutes, or until done to your liking. I prefer it medium rare. Serve hot.

PEPPER STEAK, CHINESE-STYLE

There are many variations on this dish, and I like to make it with a combination of red and green bell peppers in a black-iron skillet. I cut the peppers and onion lengthwise into canoe-shaped strips, but others may want them in squares or rings. Use round steak, flank steak, or any cut suitable for the stir-fry. Cut these against the grain into thin strips 2 or 3 inches long, more or less to match the size of the pepper and onion strips.

1 pound steak strips
1 cup hot beef stock
   (bouillon will do)
¼ cup sake, sherry, or
   dry vermouth
¼ cup peanut oil
1 red bell pepper, seeded
   and cut into slices
1 green bell pepper, seeded
   and cut into slices

1 medium onion, peeled
   and cut into slices
5 cloves garlic, peeled
3 slices gingerroot
1 tablespoon soy sauce
1 tablespoon cornstarch
salt and freshly ground
   black pepper
rice (cooked separately)

Heat the peanut oil in a cast-iron or heavy-duty skillet (or perhaps a wok). To flavor the oil, cook the garlic and gingerroot over very low heat for several minutes, until well browned, then discard. Increase the heat to medium high, and cook the steak until lightly browned, about 2 minutes. Place the steak on a heated platter. Cook the peppers and onion until the onion starts to brown nicely around the edges. Add the steak back to the skillet, along with some salt and pepper. Mix the cornstarch, soy sauce, sake, and beef stock. Pour the mixture into the skillet, stirring as you go. Bring to a boil and cook until the gravy thickens. Serve over fluffy rice. If you are eating with chopsticks, however, use that sticky short-grained rice.

STEAK FAJITAS

Many people prepare this Tex-Mex dish by cutting the meat into strips and then cooking them over a grill or in a skillet like a stir-fry, or perhaps on an oval-shaped griddle suitable for serving. There is a better way. Grill the steaks over charcoal until medium rare, then slice them into strips. This method gives a combination of texture and overall softness that goes nicely in a fajita. Also, there are all manner of marinades for the steak, but a little salt and black pepper is all you really need, if you like the flavor of beef. Often skirt steaks are used for fajitas, and these are satisfactory if they are properly sliced on a bias and not overcooked. I prefer to use thin ribeyes, grilled for only 3 minutes or so on each side before slicing.

charcoal-grilled steaks,   **chunky salsa and a selection**
  medium rare   **of go-withs**
fresh 7-inch flour tortillas

Place several fresh tortillas in aluminum foil and heat in the oven or over the grill. (If you prefer, use special tortilla containers; the main thing is to keep the tortillas moist and soft and tender.) Keep them warm while you grill the steaks. Have ready a good salsa or, better, an assortment of salsa ingredients and condiments, each in separate bowls, along with shredded lettuce. I want some chopped onions, chopped tomatoes, guacamole, shredded cheeses, salt, and freshly ground black pepper. Even cooked black beans will work. When the steaks are ready, slice them and put them on a heated skillet or griddle. Unwrap the tortillas. Top each one with steak strips and salsa, then roll it up and serve hot. Or, better, serve a tray of toppings and let each person fix his own.

CHICKEN-FRIED STEAK, TEXAS-STYLE, WITH PAN GRAVY

I normally fry chicken and chicken-fried steak using meat that has been merely dusted with flour. No batter. No chicken egg or other gook. But there are other opinions, other ways. As Linda West Eckhardt said in *The Only Texas Cookbook*, "Everyone has a favorite version of chicken-fried steak. Here is the way I like it."

1 round steak   **cooking oil**
1 chicken egg   **warm water**
flour   **salt and pepper**

Use the edge of a heavy saucer to tenderize the steak, beating it first one way and then the other, on both sides. Cut the steak into four serving pieces. Whisk the egg with a little water. Salt and pepper the steak pieces on both sides, then dredge in flour. Dip the steak pieces in egg, then again in flour. Set the steak pieces aside to allow the coating to set. Heat 1 inch of cooking oil in a skillet or Dutch oven, making it hot enough to spit back at you (Ms. Eckhardt advises). Cook the steak pieces, turning once, until browned on both sides. Turn down the heat, add 1 tablespoon of water, put on a tight-fitting lid, and cook for 5 minutes. Remove the meat (perhaps stacking the pieces onto a heated platter) and prepare the gravy.

Pour the oil out of the skillet. Scrape any bits off the bottom with a wooden spoon or wooden spatula. Put 2 tablespoons of the oil back into the skillet and add from 2 to 3 tablespoons of flour. Over low heat, cook and stir, cook and stir, until you have a golden roux. Slowly add about 1½ cups of warm water, stirring as you go, until you have a smooth gravy. Stir in some salt and pepper. Spoon a little gravy over each serving of steak. Serve with hot Texas-size biscuits, split in half and topped with gravy.

Note: Ms. Eckhardt also allows the use of warm milk instead of water to make the gravy. Suit yourself.

STEAK TARTARE FOR TWO

In *A General's Diary of Treasured Recipes,* Brigadier General Frank Dorn wrote memorably of eating steak tartare in a Chinese café (run by a German) sheltered from the wind that blew in from the Mongolian plateau. On the café walls hung mounted heads of deer, antelope, boar, and so on. The atmosphere was right for steak tartare, a dish that might well have originated from the Tartare people who allied with Genghis Khan's Mongol horde and, if I remember my Marco Polo correctly, who had a taste for raw horse meat. These days, steak tartare is usually made from very lean beef, preferably from the top sirloin section of the hind leg. Venison, being quite lean, also makes excellent steak tartare. So does buffalo.

I allow ½ pound of meat per person, but some people may not want quite that much. So, increase or decrease the measures below as required. People who live in fear of salmonella may choose to omit the raw chicken eggs from the recipe, unless they have fresh eggs from the barnyard.

1 pound freshly ground venison or lean beef	**2 tablespoons finely chopped onion**
2 chicken egg yolks (optional)	**1 tablespoon chopped parsley**
4 anchovy fillets or thin slices	**table condiments (see below)**
2 tablespoons capers	**buttered toast**

Chill or partly freeze the meat. A few minutes before serving, cut the meat into 1-inch chunks, then grind it coarsely in a sausage mill or mince it with a chef's knife. Divide the meat, mounding each half in the center of a chilled serving plate. Make a well in the center of each mound and plop in a freshly broken egg yolk. Cross two canned anchovy fillets over each mound, then surround the mound with small piles of minced onion, parsley, and capers. Each person can mix these ingredients to taste with the ground meat. Have at hand a pepper mill and salt mill loaded with sea salt, along with Worcestershire sauce, lemon quarters, cayenne pepper, prepared mustards, and so on. Serve with buttered toast. Some gourmets maintain that steak tartare goes down nicely with a little red wine. Others say that lots of wine helps.

Selecting a Beefsteak

9

IF YOU THINK you understand the various cuts of beef, stay out of French reference books on the subject. Even in America the names of the various cuts are different from region to region, city to city, and there is much abuse of terms. The larger (top loin) segment of a T-bone (without the bone), for example, is variously called a New York strip steak, a Kansas City steak, top loin steak, shell steak, strip steak, club steak, Delmonico steak, or even sirloin strip steak. Obviously, I'm not going to please everybody in this text, so I'll simply get on with what I consider to be a reasonable and workable breakdown, starting with the front shoulder of beef and working back toward the rump. I'll quickly add here that the best steaks (or at least the more tender) lie between the shoulder and the rump, variously distributed along the backbone. The same statement is true of bison, deer, moose, and most other big mammals. Why? Simply because these muscles along the backbone are not worked as much as the legs.

Following the discussions of the cuts of steak, we will get into the grades and quality of beef, discussed under several headings.

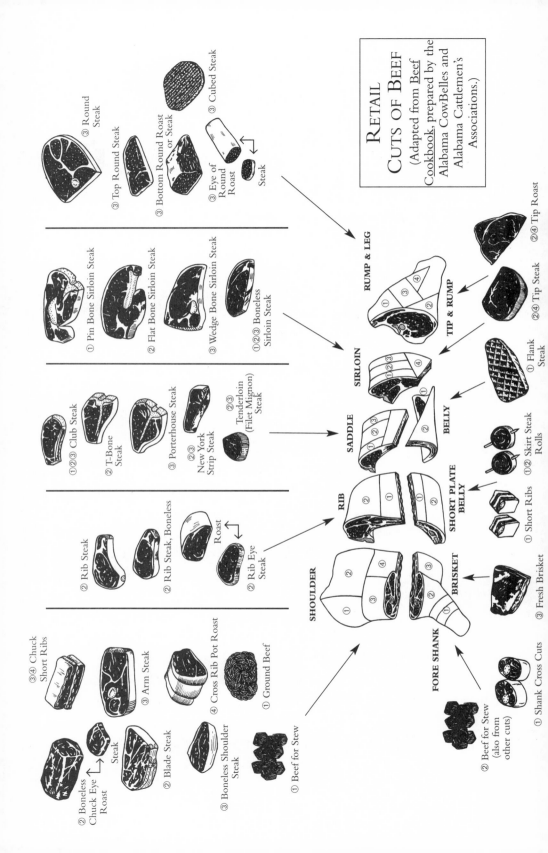

RETAIL CUTS OF BEEF
(Adapted from *Beef Cookbook*, prepared by the Alabama CowBelles and Alabama Cattlemen's Associations.)

③④ Chuck Short Ribs

② Boneless Chuck Eye Roast → Steak

② Blade Steak

③ Boneless Shoulder Steak

① Beef for Stew

③ Arm Steak

④ Cross Rib Pot Roast

① Ground Beef

② Beef for Stew (also from other cuts)

SHOULDER

FORE SHANK

② Rib Steak

② Rib Steak, Boneless Roast →

② Rib Eye Steak

RIB

BRISKET

③ Fresh Brisket

① Shank Cross Cuts

①②③ Club Steak

② T-Bone Steak

③ Porterhouse Steak

②③ New York Strip Steak

②③ Tenderloin (Filet Mignon) Steak

SADDLE

SHORT PLATE BELLY

① Short Ribs

①② Skirt Steak Rolls

① Pin Bone Sirloin Steak

② Flat Bone Sirloin Steak

③ Wedge Bone Sirloin Steak

①②③ Boneless Sirloin Steak

SIRLOIN

BELLY

① Flank Steak

③ Round Steak

③ Top Round Steak

③ Bottom Round Roast or Steak

③ Eye of Round Roast → Steak

③ Cubed Steak

RUMP & LEG

TIP & RUMP

②④ Tip Roast

②④ Tip Steak

Shoulder Beef Steaks

The front part of the beef contains the chuck, the brisket, leg shank, the neck, and other cuts. The steaks come from the chuck, which is a large chunk of meat and bone, including the brisket, weighing about 100 pounds. When the brisket is removed, it's an arm chuck. When both the arm and the brisket are removed, it's a square-cut chuck. This in turn can be cut into steaks and other cuts, or roasts and excellent ground burger meat. Unfortunately, the terminology and methods of cutting the shoulder vary so much from butcher to butcher, and from city to city, that a complete discussion here would be counterproductive. But hidden in all this is a surprise or two—and usually at a bargain price.

CHUCKEYE. At its best, this is an excellent, juicy, and tender cut of meat. It is similar to a ribeye, but a little smaller—and at half the price. The cut is sometimes called Scotch tender or Spencer. The muscle is, in fact, an extension of the ribeye muscle. In my experience, however, the quality is not dependable, even if cut by the same butcher. Technically, it is the center muscle of the chuck, but there may be some leeway. My advice is to buy chuckeyes whenever you find some that look good; then serve these to yourself and your immediate family—but not to important guests. I love chuckeyes for skillet cookery and always, when shopping the beef section of a meat counter, I search for them among the more expensive ribeye steaks.

I might add that the price of a piece of meat is not always based on quality. It's based on market demand—and the truth is that the chuck roast and chuckeye are simply not in demand like the ribeye or prime rib roast or T-bone. So, take advantage of this cut whenever you find a chuckeye that looks good. It's a nicely marbled and very juicy piece of meat. But it can be tough, so cook it in a skillet and be prepared to braise it tender. Also, be on the lookout for chuckeye roasts. These can be cut into steaks, making them as thick as you like.

BLADE STEAK. This is usually a tender cut of meat with a good flavor. It has an irregular bone structure, however, and can be tough. I like the blade steak for skillet cookery, giving me the option of long braising.

OTHER CUTS. There are several muscles in the chuck or shoulder area that can be separated and cut into steaks. Butchering schemes vary, and might include the term "under-blade steak," meaning a steak from the muscle that runs under the shoulder blade; or "top-blade steak," from the muscle that runs over the blade.

And there are several other possibilities from chuck meat. All of this meat can be used in skillet cookery, either as small steaks or cut into strips for stir-fry dishes.

So . . . why not ask your butcher for a whole shoulder, perhaps minus the brisket and the leg, and bone it out for whatever steaks you can find, using what's left for burger or stew meat? Note that the smaller muscles can be butterflied. Also, an arm steak suitable for skillet cooking followed by braising can be cut from the front leg section, bone in, like a round steak from the hind leg.

Rib Steaks

Some of the very best meat of almost any animal lies along the backbone on top of the ribs. In beef, this cut in total is usually called prime rib. It is from the small end of the rib section—from the 12th rib up toward the 7th rib, with the very best being from ribs 10 to 12. This delectable chunk of meat is what I consider to be the prime rib roast, or standing rib. (If boned, it is still a roast; if not boned, it is a standing rib roast.)

BONE-IN RIB STEAKS. This set of steaks usually comes from the 5th to the 7th or 8th ribs, after the short ribs are cut away. Being juicy, tender, and well marbled, they are perfect for grilling, broiling, or skillet cookery, if you like the bone in the meat. Unlike the single-muscle club steaks discussed under the next heading, the rib steaks actually have several muscles connected by fat and a thin membrane.

RIBEYE STEAKS. These are simply rib steaks that have the bone removed, with the best ones being cut from ribs 10 to 12. Usually, however, the ribeye is made by boning the roast and then slicing it to whatever thickness the butcher thinks will sell best. I like mine 1½ inches thick, but they are usually a little thinner in most modern markets these days. By whatever thickness, these steaks are sometimes called Delmonico steaks.

I might add that the ribeye is probably the most foolproof piece of steak available in modern markets. It is juicy, tender, and easy to carve. Use it for skillet cookery, grilling, or broiling.

The Saddle

The muscles of this large chunk of meat include the two loins or top loins that run on either side of the backbone, from the rump to the ribs—almost exactly the area that would be covered by a saddle. The cut also includes the two tenderloins, which are much smaller in diameter than the loins and are not as long, running from the rump to the club steak section, short of the ribs. With beef, the meat is usually broken down into T-bone, porterhouse, and club steaks, which are or can be further divided, as discussed under the headings below. In general, these cuts of beef are very, very good, in great demand, and priced accordingly. The same breakdown can also be used to reduce bison and large game animals. As a rule, these animals (including beef) are cut in half down the middle of the backbone, splitting the carcass from one end to the other.

Smaller animals also have pretty the same layout, but the cuts of meat are much smaller, limiting the possibilities somewhat. One rather popular cut for deer and goat is called a saddle steak, simply cut across the grain. This cut, however, is not possible after the animal has been split in half. Essentially, a saddle steak contains two loin rounds and two tenderloin rounds, with a section of the backbone in between. This same cut is also popular in alligator tail steaks.

The headings below were written primarily for beef. With veal, lamb, and other animals, the same cuts might have different names. A T-bone, for example, might be called a chop—as in pork chops.

CLUB AND DELMONICO STEAKS. These excellent steaks are cut from the small end of the loin, between the T-bones and the rib steaks. T-bones with a very small tenderloin section border on being club steaks. Usually, club steaks are sold boneless. They are also called Delmonico steaks as well as shell steaks, strip steaks, top loin, Kansas City strip steaks, New York strip steaks, and others. By whatever name, club steaks are great for broiling, grilling, or skillet cooking.

I like these steaks with the bone in, which makes for great gnawing, but they are easier to carve and eat when boneless, and they also fit better into the skillet or on the grill when cooking for a crowd.

Note that these steaks are made up of a single muscle, an extension of the loin strap that runs along the top of the T-bone and the porterhouse. It is a very good piece of meat—but not quite as good as the next set.

T-BONES. This familiar cut of beef contains a section of the loin and a section of the tenderloin. To be called a T-bone, of course, it must contain the T-shaped bone. It is best served with the bone in instead of being carved away from the table, as suggested in some recent cookbooks—which I consider to be subversive and un-American, as stated in the introduction to this work. T-bones are best when grilled or broiled, or perhaps when cooked in a skillet. I like them cut 1½ inches thick, but the typical cut as packaged in supermarkets gets thinner and thinner year by year, or so it seems. If you want a thick steak, talk to your butcher.

All T-bones from quality beef are good, but the best ones have large sections of tenderloin and border on being porterhouse steaks. The worst ones have little or no tenderloin and border on being club steaks. I seldom buy the latter type of T-bone, except when they are on sale.

Often both T-bones and porterhouse steaks, below, have a tail attached to the end. This is actually a part of the flank steak and is usually irregular or triangular in shape. It's good meat, but not as good for broiling as a T-bone. Sometimes such a steak with the tail trimmed off, and trimmed all around, is called a Kansas City. I like to use the tail and trimmings to make a beef stew.

PORTERHOUSE STEAKS. This is my favorite all-around steak. Served whole, it fills up the plate, almost, only leaving room on the small end of the steak for a baked potato and a few spears of asparagus. Porterhouse steaks should be broiled, grilled, or cooked one at a time in a skillet.

NEW YORK STRIP STEAKS. These excellent steaks are the loin part of the porterhouse or T-bone. Bewilderingly, as stated earlier, these steaks are also known top loin steaks, Kansas City steaks, loin strip steaks, shell steaks, strip steaks, club steaks, Delmonico steaks, or even sirloin strip steaks. By whatever name, these are excellent steaks for broiling, grilling, or pan-cooking. They are not as nicely marbled as the rib steaks, and not as tender as the tenderloin; but they are excellent cuts of meat when cooked rare or medium rare, helped along with good steak knives and proper carving technique (cut rather thinly, across the grain, if need be). I like a New York strip steak to be about 1½ inches thick.

Although New York strip steaks can be cut from a T-bone or porterhouse, they are usually obtained by a different process. The whole loin is cut out, and this is cut into strip steaks, whereas T-bones and Porterhouse steaks are cut across the bone. This same comment also applies to the tenderloin, below, which is usually cut thicker than a T-bone or porterhouse because it is smaller in diameter.

TENDERLOIN. These choice strips of meat run parallel under the saddle, one on either side of the backbone, extending from the rump to the ribs. Each tenderloin is rather conical and tapers from the porterhouse end of the saddle to the club steak section of the saddle. Some of the several sirloin steaks contain a round of the tenderloin.

About 18 inches long and weighing in at 4 to 6 pounds, the tenderloins can be removed whole during the butchering process. These can be used as a roast for such dishes as beef Wellington, or they can be cut into small steaks, as indicated in the next headings.

Châteaubriand. This highly prized piece of meat is the center of the tenderloin and is usually cut 2 or 3 inches thick. It is cooked whole, not butterflied.

Filet mignon. These are cut usually smaller in diameter than the châteaubriand and can vary considerably in size. This cut is often wrapped in bacon. But not everything that is wrapped in bacon is a real filet mignon, and the bacon was probably used from the outset to hold a butterflied filet mignon (cut from the smaller end) together. I might add that I really like my filet mignon wrapped in bacon, especially for skillet cooking.

Tournedos. These steaks are usually cut from the small end of the tenderloin. Often they are cut on the bias to make them larger. They can also be cut across the grain and butterflied.

SADDLE STEAKS. This large steak is a cross-cut of the saddle and looks like two T-bones or porterhouses joined, which is exactly what it is. The steak is not common, partly because of the practical custom of cutting beef in half along the backbone during the primary butchering process.

Belly Steaks

The side and underside of large animals contain thin, fibrous muscles that can be trimmed into steaks or used as burger meat. With beef, such steaks include the flank steak and the skirt steak. I don't consider the beef brisket, or bottom of the breast, to be of steak quality, but I'll have to add that corned beef and cabbage is one of my favorite dishes, provided that I can find corned beef that isn't too fatty. I also like a brisket cooked slowly over charcoal, using the indirect method, with plenty of smoke.

FLANK STEAKS. Often called London broil steak, this cut of beef is rather uniformly thin, not unlike a slab of bacon. When trimmed, it weighs about 2 or 2½ pounds. It is often broiled or grilled, then thinly carved on a bias. The idea is to cut the long, tough muscle into thin slices. If cooked and carved properly, flank steaks are quite tasty and easily eaten. If overcooked or improperly carved, the meat is difficult to chew. When serving flank as steaks, provide your guests with good, sharp steak knives.

In addition to London broil, the flank steak is often used for dishes that call for thin slices—Asian stir-fry dishes, Chinese pepper steak, fajitas, and so on. The flank is also butterflied (folded out like a book) and stuffed. As often as not, these stuffed steaks are baked. Sometimes, flank steaks are tenderized mechanically, trimmed, rolled, pinned with toothpicks, and billed as "pinwheel tenderloin."

SKIRT STEAKS. These beltlike steaks are actually the diaphragm muscles (two on each animal) that control breathing. These days, skirt steaks are usually used in the restaurant trade for making fajitas. Even if found in consumer meat markets, they are priced too high for what you get—flavorful but somewhat tough. They are usually grilled or pan-broiled, then cut *across the grain* into thin strips for fajitas. The skirt steak is also rolled, pinned with toothpicks, and billed as a skirt tenderloin.

Sirloin and Rump

These chunks of meat lie at the end of the backbone, containing part of the hipbone and the interior section of the tailbone. There is much that could be said about steaks from this area—too much, really, for the quality of the eating. I'll try to keep it short.

SIRLOIN. This part of the beef, as I define it, lies between the porterhouse section of the backbone and the rump. A lot goes on in here in terms of muscle and bone, so that the chunk of meat yields several sirloin steaks, such as pinbone, flat-bone, full-cut, wedgebone, and short sirloin. The section joining the porterhouse steaks also contains a round of the tenderloin. Most of the true sirloins are large steaks, weighing up to 4 or 4½ pounds when only 1½ inches thick. Often they are divided into smaller steaks, further confusing the issue. Even the term "sirloin" itself is confusing, being applied to the New York strip section of loin and to a large irregular muscle from the hind leg (sirloin tip).

In general, sirloin steak can be very good—and sometimes not so good. I have read that the first slice of steak between the porterhouse and the rest of the sirloin is not a good choice because of some tendons in the meat. Sirloin is almost always grilled, often by men and good ol' boys of gourmand intent, bent on buying simply the biggest steak in the store. According to George Leonard Herter, a man of firm opinion, the sirloin is seldom eaten by women and should always be aged before eating!

According to me: Be careful with anything called sirloin or sirloin tip. If you have a choice of several sirloins, choose one with a long, flat center bone.

I almost always use a tenderizing marinade with a sirloin, usually containing citrus or a little papaya juice.

RUMP. This chunk of beef, usually used in roasts, sits atop the leg muscles and behind the sirloin proper. It is sometimes sliced into steaks, but I don't recommend them, partly because it's difficult to know what's what. There is some confusion between the sirloin and the rump, and such terms as "bottom sirloin." All this will never be cut-and-dried as long as the U.S. Department of Agriculture allows so many cuts of beef to be labeled by the retailer, but for sanity's sake I draw a clear picture of the rump: a triangular chunk of meat, containing part of the hipbone, between the sirloin proper and the leg round—clearly separating the true sirloin from the "sirloin tip" section of the leg.

Leg Round

A cross section cut from the rear leg is known as round steak, featuring a round leg bone (femur) in the center. During these days of small meat portions, it is cut rather thin, ½ to 1 inch, and is seldom packaged whole. Instead it is divided into sections, usually according to the natural divisions of its four muscles, as shown in the drawing. (A fifth muscle, the heel of round, doesn't show in cross section and isn't important as a steak.) Although different in terms of tenderness, texture, and fat content, all of these cuts are suitable for country steak or chicken-fried steak, or for recipes calling for long simmering. (Remember, however, that long, slow simmering does not mean boiling. Boiling round steak can actually make it tougher.) These steaks should not be cooked by direct radiant heat such as grilling or broiling.

On the other hand, round steak is very, very flavorful when fried in a skillet and then smothered and simmered in a gravy. In fact, round steak might well be the favorite cut of beef in some country households. I confess that I, a country boy, had to go to college for several years before I began to appreciate the merits of a medium-rare T-bone properly grilled over charcoal. Back then, grilling over coals wasn't very popular. People cooked in the house, if possible, and round steak properly simmered in a cast-iron skillet was a favorite. It still is in some families.

ROUND
STEAK

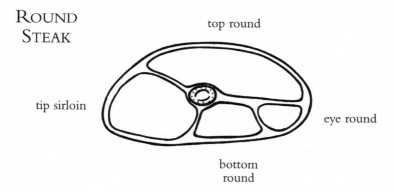

top round

tip sirloin

eye round

bottom
round

The drawing above shows the layout of the muscles in a leg of beef. If you buy a round steak at the supermarket these days, remember that it will not often contain all of the cross section. If you have a choice, avoid the bottom round, which is quite fibrous.

TIP SIRLOIN. Also known as silver tip and knuckle-face, this irregular piece of meat, 13 to 14 pounds of it, is best cooked slowly as a roast. The meat has a fine texture and works best when barded. The sirloin tip is sometimes sliced 1½ or 2 inches thick for a London broil, or ½ inch for country steak.

In any case, the cut is not really a sirloin and should be billed at market under another name, I firmly declare.

TOP ROUND. This large chunk of meat, 18 to 22 pounds after trimming, has a fine grain. When sliced to appropriate thicknesses and
widths, it is a good source of meat for London broil, country steak,
Chinese pepper steak, cube steaks, and so on. Top round, partly
because it is a large chunk of meat, is often the choice cut for steak
tartare and ground beef to be eaten as steak tartare (chapter 8).

EYE OF ROUND. This long cylinder of meat, about 6 pounds in all,
looks better than it eats. Being tough, it is best when sliced about ½
inch thick, well beaten every which way, and used in country steak
recipes. The meat works best with long, slow simmering in a skillet.

BOTTOM ROUND. Also called the rump and the gooseneck, this large
chunk of meat, about 14 pounds, works best as a pot roast. It contains more tough fibers in the meat. I don't recommend this cut for
use as a steak, unless it is pounded thoroughly for use in a country
steak recipe calling for long, slow simmering in gravy.

Grades of Beef

All commercial beef is graded at the slaughterhouse by the U.S.
Department of Agriculture at government expense and carries an
official stamp of approval, which supposedly certifies that the animal
was healthy and suitable for human consumption. At the meatpack-
er's expense, the USDA will also grade the beef—but this is not
required by current law.

There are problems and conflicts with grading beef in the modern world. People who relish well-marbled meat may put a premium
on that quality, whereas sticklers for a low-fat diet will prefer a leaner meat. Moreover, the grading system changes from time to time.
For all practical purposes, however, the grading system is a guide for
the wholesaler and retailer instead of for the consumer. Some of the
lower of several grades of beef are seldom packaged as steaks or other
cuts; instead they are used in frankfurters and so on.

The top of the grades—prime beef—represents only about 4
percent of the beef processed in this country. This cut seldom gets

into supermarkets or neighborhood meat markets. Instead, it goes to swanky restaurants, private clubs, and fancy meat markets. It is expensive and is often aged, as discussed in the next section.

Most of the steaks sold in supermarkets are graded "choice" or "U.S. Choice," although those words may or may not appear on the package. About 20 percent of the total output of beef is graded "choice." But there is a wide range in this category, and sometimes you might see the designation of "top choice." This wide range might explain the variations in the quality of steaks from day to day in supermarkets, or from steak to steak on any given day. But, again, the steaks are not required by law to carry a "choice" rating, and many will carry a brand name instead.

Clearly, the consumer who knows a little about beef will sometimes be able to select better steaks simply by looking at them in the market display. As a rule, the better steaks will have a bright pink color with thin lines of white fat spiderwebbing the meat. This network of fat is called marbling, and this is what makes the meat tender and succulent. Little pockets of fat and uneven, coarse marbling reduce the quality of the meat.

So, look at what you are getting. With a good eye and a little luck, you might even pick up a prime steak at regular price.

Dry-Aged Beef

Beef, bison, and venison that has been properly aged (or hung) for two or three weeks has more flavor and better texture. Always, it's best to age large chunks of meat—a quarter or a half of the animal—with the fat still attached to the surface. The meat should be hung at a temperature of about 35 degrees in an environment of low humidity. This is called dry-aging. In addition to the time and space required to age meat in this manner, there is a considerable weight loss—up to 20 percent—caused by evaporation and trimming the surface of the meat, which becomes dry and sometimes moldy during the process. A steak cut from a dry-aged beef has a redder color, more concentrated flavor, and a firmer texture than unaged beef—but at the same time, owing to an enzymeic action on the cells, it is more tender than regular market beef.

In any case, aged beef is simply not widely available these days in most markets. And drying beef at home is not practical unless a large walk-in meat cooler, or perhaps an old refrigerator, is available. If you want to age your own, start with a large chunk of freshly butchered beef with the outer fat still attached (the fat is necessary for the process to work properly), hang it at 35 degrees, and leave it alone for two weeks. It may or may not fulfill your expectations, depending on the quality of the animal.

Feedlot beef is quite different from range beef, and aging won't change that fact. Most of us still want a fat beef with nicely marbled flesh, but the trend is toward a leaner meat for reasons of health. Ironically, the old Texas longhorns may turn out to be better than the fancy black Angus or whiteface Hereford for producing range-run steaks, and I understand there is a move afoot in Texas to promote them.

In any case, people who become accustomed to supermarket fare may not like the more intense flavor of expensive dry-aged beef.

"Wet-Aged" Beef

These days, most aged beef is said to be "wet-aged," in which it is vacuum-packed in polyethylene bags. In this case, the meat develops a wet surface film instead of drying. Holding the vacuum-packed meat under refrigeration for two or three weeks will indeed improve the texture and flavor, but these days it is usually shipped directly from the processor to the supermarket, distributor, or retail meat market, aging along the way. It may or may not be aged more than a few days. In some cases, the meat that arrives at a supermarket will be reduced to T-bones, wrapped in plastic, and put out for sale within hours of arrival. Note that reducing the carcass to steaks and other cuts ends the true aging process.

In any case, most meats are vacuum-packed in plastic or in boxes (Cry-O-Vac) of 70 pounds or a little less at the slaughterhouse, then shipped to the meat market or supermarket. This leaves the meat markets without much control over what they get, and is a far and sad cry from the old days when a butcher could select his own beef from rows of carcasses hanging in a cooler.

Feedlot vs. Range Cattle

Most of the beef sold in America is shipped on the hoof from the ranch to a feedlot operation, usually located in a big grain-producing area such as Iowa. The animals are fed heavily in a restricted area, permitting them little exercise and thereby causing them to put on meat and fat. I think the meat is softer and probably more tender than a range animal, free to walk and romp and exercise, but this doesn't necessarily mean that the meat is better. It depends on your thinking.

The practice of fattening animals for the slaughter is very old, going back at least to the Romans. At first such pampered meat was for the very rich. In America, the practice became widespread during the days of the great cattle drives. Think about it. If a scrawny range animal was driven overland from west Texas to Dodge City, then loaded onto a train and shipped to Chicago for butchering, it really needed some time in a feedlot to become edible. If the same animal were killed and processed back on the ranch and dry-aged for a couple of weeks, it would probably make very good eating and would be lower in fat. If it were fed some corn back on the ranch before the slaughter, so much the better. It would be easier and more humane, it seems to me, to ship the corn to the ranch than to ship the live animal to the corn.

Times are slowly changing, and I hope to see more and more small, local meat processors around the country. This trade is restricted, however, by the USDA, and a few years back a lot of small operators were forced out of business because of one regulation or another. This tended to bunch all our beef up at a few big processors around the country. The problem with big meat operations, it seems to me, is similar to the bad apple spoiling the whole barrel. Under the eye of the USDA we now have large batches of salmonella chicken and *E. coli* hamburger making newspaper headlines from time to time.

But the way back to range cattle for the masses will not be quick. Even farmers and ranchers buy their steaks in the supermarkets these days. Still, my vote goes to range cattle. The meat will be firmer, not only because of less fat but also because of more exercise. It will also have more flavor. The same is true of chicken and turkey. And it's a more humane approach.

Frozen Beef

I often buy steaks at the supermarket and freeze them at home. Sometimes I freeze the package as is, usually with the meat displayed in little Styrofoam trays and topped with stretch-it plastic, but it's better to wrap the package again with freezer paper or aluminum foil. Sometimes I remove the steaks and wrap them more tightly. Usually, home-frozen steaks should be eaten within a month or two. The new home vacuum-pack systems will keep steaks even longer. When freezing meat at home, remember that the ideal freezing temperature is about −30 degrees, whereas the coldest you can hope for in most home units is 0 to 5 degrees. The idea is to freeze the meat as quickly as possible. It helps to freeze only a small amount at a time. So, if you buy a whole loin or rib section of beef and have it cut into steaks, keep the meat in a cooler and freeze a few steaks at a time.

Commercially frozen steaks—vacuum-packed and quick-frozen at a very low temperature—will keep almost indefinitely provided that they are not thawed and refrozen.

Steaks can be thawed or partly thawed and refrozen safely, within reason, but it will suffer in quality, tending to be dry and tasteless.

To thaw steaks, it's best to loosen the package and thaw the contents in the refrigerator. Thawing the meat at room temperature will cause some of the juices to run out. Remember that thawing in the refrigerator will take much longer, and some of us are guilty of forcing the issue by running water over the packaged steak or using the microwave.

The better way, if you don't have time to thaw the meat in the refrigerator, is simply to put the frozen steaks directly on the grill, under the broiler, or in the skillet. The cooking will take longer, depending partly on the thickness, and the finished product will be well done on the outside and rare or medium rare in the center. It's best to cut into the steak in the thickest part (away from the bone) to check for doneness before serving, unless you have lots of experience with cooking frozen steaks. I don't object to cooking properly frozen steaks, and I find them exciting or somewhat daring.

Finally, remember that it's much safer to eat meat that has been frozen for two weeks or longer at 0 degrees or lower. Freezing kills most harmful bacteria and parasites. This point can be especially important for those of us who like medium-rare steaks, and for the brave few who relish raw beef dishes such as steak tartare.

OTHER STEAKS AND A CHOP OR TWO

10

A NUMBER OF THE world's larger animals provide meat that can be cut and cooked like steaks. Alligator tail steaks, for example, are very good when marinated with a little lemon juice and broiled over charcoal, helped along with a baste of lemon juice and melted butter. We can't cover everything in this book, but, for cooking purposes, I consider all these creatures fair game.

The only requirement for a steak, from my view, is that the meat be cut to a suitable thickness, across the grain, and be large enough to interest a hungry nonvegan. If the meat is cut with the grain, the whole texture is different, although a few cuts go this route. A flank steak, for example, is of necessity cut into a steak with the grain—but then it should be thinly cut across the grain before eating it. Also, a Nubian steak (difficult to find these days) goes back to the time when some primitive peoples cut a slab of meat off the hind leg of a domestic animal. This provided a little meat for the table, while still keeping the animal for milk or calving.

In any case, here are some alternatives to beef that may be of interest for one reason or another. I might add that the best meats are not necessarily what the world eats at the present time. American buffalo, for example, might well be the best meat for steaking, but the animal is difficult to control in captivity and it simply wasn't suitable for the early roundups and cattle drives (or shipping via railroad or modern trucks) to the corn belt feedlots and population centers. In the future, we may see a shift away from feedlot beef and toward a leaner range-fed meat. In time, perhaps buffalo or ostrich will become the meat of choice in America. But the old ways die slowly, except in times of famine, and the new ways are led for the most part by rich people who can afford ostrich and buffalo.

In any case, here is my take on some alternative steaks, beginning with the familiar.

Pork

The better cuts of pork have pretty much the same configuration as for beef, only smaller. As a rule, good pork comes from animals that are four or five months old and weigh 200 pounds or a little better. Yes, pigs do produce lots of fat, but the lean cuts of pork, well trimmed, aren't any fatter than beef and may be even leaner.

The big problem for those of us who like rare or medium-rare meat is that fresh pork should be cooked well done to negate the trichina parasite, which embeds itself in the flesh and can cause trichinosis in humans. Pork chops and steaks can be successfully grilled, broiled, or cooked in a skillet, but the methods require long, slow cooking, usually at a lower temperature. The USDA advises that an internal temperature of 160 degrees Fahrenheit will kill trichina. Most experts agree that freezing the meat at 0 degrees or colder for several weeks (at least three) will make fresh pork safe to eat with less cooking.

The fully cooked "cured" pork, including hams and shoulders, are a little safer and are often very good. Try smoked pork chops grilled over charcoal. Center-cut hams are also nice for grilling or broiling.

The fully cured hams, sometimes called country hams, are too dry and hard and salty to cook as steaks or chops, although some people like to slice them and cook them in a skillet. These salt-cured hams are best when soaked in fresh water (with several changes) and then cooked in a liquid. Of course, country ham fried in a skillet has a wonderful (albeit salty) flavor and makes good redeye gravy, but it's really not the stuff for a book about steaks.

In any case, here are the better cuts of fresh pork for cooking as steaks:

CENTER-CUT LOIN CHOPS. These look exactly like T-bone and porterhouse steaks from beef, only smaller. The best ones have a large eye of tenderloin. Often, center loin will be boned and the two muscles cut into boneless loin chops (or roast) and tenderloin. Both the tenderloin and the top loin are sold in strips. These can be purchased whole and sliced to whatever thickness you want. And remember that the tenderloin (sometimes called Canadian bacon) can easily be butterflied, making a small but choice steak.

RIB CHOPS. These are almost as good as center-cut loin chops, but they have no tenderloin round. They can be purchased with or without the bone. Those with the bone can be Frenched, in which the meat and fat are cut away from the rib, making it look like a handle.

HIP CHOPS. Sometimes called pork steaks or loin end chops, these are similar to sirloin cuts in beef. They are good in flavor, but have an irregular bone structure, just as sirloin beef does.

SHOULDER CHOPS. These have lots of fat and broad bones. Tasty, though, and tender.

HAM STEAKS. These can be cut from either the shank end or the butt end of the hind-leg ham. Your butcher may not want to cut these for you unless you buy the whole ham or half a half, which is the way most fresh pork is sold these days. Cured ham steaks are often available, but almost always they are too thin for culinary comfort. Buy a whole ham and ask your butcher to cut it for you on special order.

ARM STEAKS. Cut from the thicker part of front leg, these are not as good as ham steaks, but they are usually much cheaper. Purchase a whole shoulder and have your butcher cut it for you.

BLADE STEAKS. These are cut from the butt end of the pork shoulder, sometimes called Boston butt, and often contain lots fat and gristle as well as bone.

Lamb and Mutton

In this country, lamb meat comes from a young sheep, under one year of age. The meat of older sheep is known as mutton. In the United States, lamb is not very popular in some areas—and mutton is not even acknowledged in most books and magazines, or on TV cooking shows. Mutton has a stronger flavor and should not be served to people who are uncertain about lamb.

Much of the lamb sold in the United States is imported from New Zealand and other countries. The best domestic lamb is butchered when it is five or six months old, and is known in meat trade as spring lamb or early lamb. The USDA grades lamb as "prime," "choice," and "good," based in large part (but not exclusively) on size or weight. Baby lamb, sometimes bottle-fed, is considered prime eating, but it is difficult to find and expensive. In most markets, the lamb will be "choice" grade. If you have a selection to choose from, look for meat that has a bright pink color with pure white fat. The better cuts of lean meat, such as loin chops, will have smooth, firm texture with a fine, barely perceptible marbling.

Generally, lamb chops and steaks are ideal for cooking over charcoal. They are at their best when cooked rare or medium rare, like beef—but lamb and mutton should be cooked a little slower. Ideally, the chops should be cut at least 1½ inches thick, then broiled or grilled until brown on the outside and nicely pink on the inside. Be warned that the fat from the larger animals, and especially from mutton, is not tasty and should be trimmed away before cooking.

LOIN CHOPS. These correspond to T-bones and porterhouse beef steaks. The meat is tender and succulent, but the chops should be trimmed by the butcher or by the cook. I prefer them 1½ inches thick for broiling, and perhaps a little thinner for cooking in a skillet.

ENGLISH CHOPS. Cut from the saddle in cross section, these resemble two porterhouse or T-bone steaks jammed together, with the whole backbone in the center. Often cut 2½ or 3 inches thick, they are perfect for cooking slowly over charcoal, until just pink in the center. Grill these for true meat lovers, serving up a whole chop per plate.

RIB CHOPS. These are cut from the front part of the loin and the ribs, and they range widely in quality. Those close to the shoulder may not be of top quality, but generally rib chops are very good. They are usually sold bone in, which makes them cook quicker and provides some excellent gnawing. Frenched chops have the fat and meat trimmed from the bone on the small end.

Usually, I allow at least two chops for each person. I can eat another one or two.

SIRLOIN CHOPS. These are cut from the rump section of the lamb, and are irregular in shape. They have an excellent flavor, however, and are nice to broil or cook in a skillet.

LAMB ROUND STEAKS. These are cut from the hind leg, similar to a beef round steak. They can be cooked like a steak, but they are not as tender as the loin cuts; still, they are very, very good when rubbed with olive oil and garlic and cooked to perfection, rather slowly, over charcoal. In most markets, these will not be marketed as steaks but as a whole leg. I highly recommend that you buy a leg and have the butcher cut out some steaks from the center, making them at least an inch thick. Save the rest for Irish stew or some such recipe.

SHOULDER CHOPS. The arm chops and blade chops are cut from the shoulder end of the lamb. Often you'll have to purchase a whole shoulder to get at these, but your butcher should cut them for you. Save the rest for stew meat and kabobs.

Veal and Baby Beef

I don't hold veal in high esteem as a source of steaks or chops. Lacking in robust flavor, it lends itself to sauced recipes or something like breaded veal cutlets or veal scaloppine, or cooked by braising or stewing. With the possible exception of loin or rib cuts, this meat should not be grilled or broiled. Generally, the meat is a product of the dairy industry, not the meat industry per se, and is from the calves of such milk cows as Holsteins. Technically, the term can cover unborn calves and those up to three months old, or even older. The older calves are sometimes marketed as baby beef, but they don't have the flavor of fully grown beef. In either case, the meat is simply too expensive for what you get, I think. People who purchase veal or baby beef expecting a juicy, tender steak may be sorely disappointed. Instead, it may in turn out to be dry, tough, and tasteless.

In any case, veal is graded by the USDA as "prime," "choice," and "good." Almost all the steaks and chops available in regular retail outlets are "choice." The "prime" goes to swanky restaurant trade and the "good" goes into ground meat, baby food, and other products. In a prime veal steak or cutlet, the lean meat will be pink to grayish white with very little fat or marbling. Its texture is fine grained. Here are some common cuts:

LOIN CHOPS. These are really miniature T-bones and porterhouses, and look accordingly, except for sizes. (I have also seen larger ones sold as baby beef T-bones.) Sometimes fancy loin chops are sold with a part of the kidney attached, rolled in and secured by a strip of the flank section. These are called kidney chops. A true loin chop, of course, will have part of the tenderloin as well as the top loin. On the larger veal, the loins may be boned out, sliced, and marketed as scallops.

RIB CHOPS. These are similar to rib steaks in beef.

VEAL CUTLETS OR VEAL LEG CUTLETS. The steaks cut from the shoulder or hind leg of veal are sometimes called cutlets. Also, the larger leg muscles are sometimes separated, cut into rounds, and marketed as scallops.

Venison

Deer, elk, caribou, moose, and similar animals make excellent red meat, lean and tasty, if they are properly handled. The so-called gamey flavor is not natural in prime, healthy animals. It is the hunter's responsibility to bring home a prime animal, quickly killed with a well-placed shot, and promptly field-dressed. The real purpose of field-dressing, I might explain, is not to remove the innards per se, but to remove the heat they contain and to open the body cavity for ventilation.

These days lots of venison is being raised on game farms and marketed through specialty meat shops, by mail, and over the Internet. If properly handled, it is good, low-fat, red meat. Once in the cook's hand, venison must not be overcooked by any dry heat method. Rare or medium rare is by far the best, unless the steak will be cooked au jus or simmered in gravy.

The more tender steaks and chops come from along the backbone or loin section. T-bones, fillet, top loin, and rib chops are similar to beef. Round steaks cut from the hind leg are also good, if properly cooked. Hunters and home butchers should know that the tenderest part—the tenderloin—can be removed during the field-dressing or butchering process. These, one on either side of the backbone, are clearly visible and are easily cut away from the backbone as soon as the innards are removed and before the animal has been skinned. (The tenderloins almost pull away without cutting.) The strip of meat can be butterflied and cooked like a steak without aging. The larger cuts—hams, saddle, shoulder—should, for best results, be aged before reducing them to steaks or roasts. (See the previous chapter for notes on aging beef.)

There is, of course, some difference in the flavor of the various deer-type animals, and, in some cases, the flavor is influenced by what the animal has been eating—and on the condition of rut. Personally,

I welcome the variations, and I have eaten everything from white-tailed deer to musk-ox. But frankly, the care of the meat before cooking and the cooking itself are more important than the kind of venison.

Bear

The black bear has made a comeback in America. Several states now offer hunting, and the meat is sometimes available from retail outlets that traffic in game and unusual fare. In times past, the meat was highly regarded in parts of northern Europe, and in Russia bear hams are sometimes cured like pork. Although the loin or leg round steaks can be very tasty when grilled, they may be a little tough. More importantly, bear, like pork, can harbor the trichina parasite, and this fact complicates and restricts the safe cooking of the steaks. See the note under fresh pork earlier in this chapter.

Buffalo or Bison

The American buffalo might well make the best T-bone steak I've ever eaten. My first one came from a small café in Winters, Texas, some years ago, long before buffalo farming became a popular hobby for rich people. At the time I was a travel editor with *Southern Living Magazine,* and, naturally, I wrote an article on the subject. The owner of the eatery wrote me an urgent letter, printed in block letters, thanking me for the article but asking me not to write anymore about his business. He explained that people had come into Winters from all over the country and had "et every buffalo" in that part of the country.

In any case, American buffalo is a rich red meat with a slightly sweet taste. It needs no improvement, except for a little salt. I will also allow some black pepper, if it be freshly ground.

Generally, the cuts of meat described in the beefsteak chapter will apply to buffalo. The hump is very good bonus eating. Ground buffalo, by the way, makes wonderful burgers.

These days, buffalo meat is becoming available in more and more markets and restaurants, and by mail, or over the Internet. Be sure to order some T-bone steaks at least 1½ inches thick. Grill them over hot charcoal or wood coals.

The American buffalo is really a bison. The real buffalo of Africa and Asia also makes good meat, but is seldom available in this country. At one time, experiments were being made with raising these in the marshy flatlands of south Florida, but I haven't as yet seen any of the meat on the market.

Other similar animals grow here and there around the world, such as the yak in high Tibet. The musk-ox of the far north, by the way, is really a big goat, not a buffalo or ox. The meat tastes good enough, but it can be on the tough side.

Ostrich, Emu, and Rhea

In recent years there has been much speculation with ostrich and emu farms and brood stock as well as with the smaller rhea from South America. The belief was that these big birds—good red meat low in marbled fat—would be demanded in our markets as a substitute for beef. It hasn't happened, and I suspect that the market price of eggs and brood stock has crashed. But the meat is good and it is available in specialty markets, by mail, and on the Internet. It should be consumed for its own sake, not as a substitute for anything else.

There is some confusion about what's what, and we clearly lack the terms "T-bone" and "ribeye." Some of the best steaks are simply a cross section from the thigh, but standard cuts or names have not become well established. The best bet is to ask your supplier what's what from the price list—but the chances are good that whomever you are talking with won't know, either. So, try cuts shaped like a steak or chop, at least an inch thick, preferably thicker. Cook these just as you would beefsteaks of the same thickness, but I would suggest that you cook them in a skillet—and be ready to resort to plan B if the meat turns out to be tough. That is, be prepared to simmer the steaks in their own gravy for an hour or longer.

I suspect that an investigation into native African, Australian, and South American cookery would reveal some interesting recipes for these big, flightless birds. In the Argentine, for example, a classic recipe for rhea steaks, presumably cut from the thigh, requires that they be first wrapped around a hot stone, which aids in the cooking. Native African recipes for ostrich and other meats are not easy to come by, partly because most of the "authentic" cookbooks and magazine articles are greatly Americanized, and most editors simply don't want to talk about saddle steaks of chimpanzee.

I have some emu recipes from Australia, where the birds are now farmed commercially and are still hunted in the bush, but most of these call for ingredients not readily available to me (such as native pepper leaves or dried akudjura). My mouth waters, however, for a recipe called Kangaroo and Emu Steaks with Two Fruit Sauces, as published in the *Australia the Beautiful Cookbook*. The same book also sets forth recipes for crocodile steaks, which would surely be good with American alligators, and for wild buffalo steaks from the Outback. I suspect these are from feral animals, either water buffalo or American bison or both. The book doesn't say which. Nor does it mention camel, which I understand has got loose and grows wild on the continent.

Fish Steaks

Most fish steaks are cut from large fish, 10 pounds or better, and are cut across the backbone. Meats sliced off the side are fillets, not true steaks. Either can be cooked like a steak, but there is often a lot of difference in texture—even from the same fish.

Firm fish steaks can be grilled or broiled like beefsteaks, but flaky ones (and especially flaky fillets) work best in a wire grilling basket. I'm not offering many fish recipes in this book, but I'll say here that one of my favorite methods is very simple. Spread some good mayonnaise over both sides of a very fresh fish steak and broil it close to the heat for a few minutes on each side. The general rule: Cook both steaks and fillets for a total of 10 minutes per inch of thickness. Steaks, being of uniform thickness if cut by a sober butcher, work nicely on a grill or under the broiler, whereas fillets tend to taper. One solution is to cut large fillets across the grain into uniform strips of an inch or more, then roll these into wheels and pin them with skewers or round toothpicks. This will give you a "pinwheel steak" of uniform thickness and the "across the grain" texture. I like to brush the skin side heavily with bacon drippings before rolling the fillets.

Tuna, billfish, salmon, and others are being marketed as steaks these days. Personally, I put more stock in freshness and proper handling than in species.

Go-Withs

11

I AM NOT STRICTLY a meat-and-potatoes man. But, frankly, as made clear in the introduction to this little book, I don't get very excited about pasta with a big porterhouse on the plate and I don't really want any damned beans with my T-bone, either, thank you ma'am. What I look for is something unusual and special, along with the mundane potato.

Here are a few suggestions.

Salads and Their Dressing

I always enjoy a good green salad served at any time during the meal. But I really don't want to fill myself up on a huge Greek salad before I tackle the steak. Also, I like to serve the salad as a side dish along with the steak, and a simple salad seems to work best.

Many people in this country serve the salad before the steak, and our restaurants have sold us on this bill of fare. Their idea is to serve you something to keep you busy while the steak cooks, and some restaurants these days direct you to a salad bar. My idea, however, is to forget the soup course and hold the salad until the steak is ready to eat.

If the salad is to be served separately from the main meal, I suggest that you hold it until after the steaks have been eaten. This lightens things up and sets the way for dessert. This practice is proper, by the way, in some time-honored continental menus.

In any case, here are a few of my own salad suggestions, along with a dressing or two. I try to avoid the heavy cream-type dressings and cheese dressings when serving steak—but suit yourself.

OIL AND VINEGAR

My favorite all-around salad dressing is simply extra-virgin olive oil and a good red wine vinegar, served in separate bottles. I also enjoy a shake bottle with spices mixed with oil and vinegar, as in zesty Italian.

VINAIGRETTE—A SPARSE RECIPE

Here's a basic recipe for a premixed salad dressing. If you use good oil with lots of flavor of the olive in it and a good red wine vinegar, other ingredients, except for a touch of prepared mustard, will not be needed.

1 cup extra-virgin olive oil	**1 tablespoon Dijon mustard**
2 tablespoons red wine vinegar	**freshly ground sea salt to taste**

In a suitable bowl, whisk the vinegar, mustard, and sea salt. Pour in the olive oil slowly, in a small stream, whisking as you go. Whisk until the mixture emulsifies. It's best to store vinaigrette in a jar or bottle with a tightly fitting lid, then shake it before serving.

TOMATO AND VIDALIA SALAD

I like to use Vidalia onions for this salad, but any large, mild white onion will do. If you must guess, the very mild onions tend to be flat, not football shaped. Also, use large, very ripe tomatoes. I like

Cherokee purples, which I grow in my garden. Although this tomato doesn't keep very long (making it unsuitable for supermarket dis-
tribution), it has a very good flavor and an unusual red-and-purple
streaked color.

To serve, alternate slices of tomatoes and onions on a serving
platter. Border with slices of bell pepper, if desired, or mild banana
peppers. Serve homemade mayonnaise in small bowls, and have a
pepper mill and sea salt at hand. Or, if you prefer, have ready olive oil
and vinegar.

JÍCAMA WITH PAPAYA SEEDS

The jícama, a root vegetable from Mexico, is now being grown in
the warmer areas of the United States and is available in most
supermarkets that have an international produce section. The root
looks somewhat like a turnip, but the texture and taste resemble
water chestnuts, making them good additions to a quickly cooked
stir-fry. I like jícama sliced and served raw as a salad, garnished with
lemon or lime wedges and sprinkled lightly with cayenne. For a
memorable contrast in color and flavor, try garnishing a small platter of sliced jícama with the peppery, shiny, jet black seeds of the
papaya fruit.

If you have any leftover seeds (and a papaya has lots of 'em
inside), refrigerate them until needed in another context—or dry and
grind them in a mill like peppercorns. The seeds, ground or crushed,
are sometimes used in salad dressings or marinades.

HEARTS OF PALM SALAD

Sometimes called swamp cabbage and millionaire's salad (depending
on whether you partake in the Big Scrub area of Florida or in a
swanky restaurant in Manhattan), the hearts or cores of some young
palm trees make a very good vegetable or salad. These can be gathered from the wild, but remember that a whole tree must be
destroyed in order to get a salad. Years ago, I bought some palm
rounds from a country store in Perry, Florida, and fresh swamp cab-

bage may still be available here and there. In any case, it can be purchased in most supermarkets these days under the name hearts of palm, usually canned in Brazil or somewhere in Central America. The canned product has been cooked and can be served hot or cold. The fresh kind can be served raw or cooked. The heart of the palm is beautifully white, but when raw it will turn yellow if exposed to the air. If you are lucky enough to have freshly peeled palm hearts, keep them in water until time to cook or serve.

If you are using canned swamp cabbage, you'll find four to six logs about 1 inch in diameter. Simply remove the logs from the can, rinse them, and carefully slice them into ¼- to ½-inch wheels. Serve these on individual salad plates garnished with lemon wedges or top with a salad dressing.

I have eaten swamp cabbage in Florida restaurants with all manner of stuff in them, including a dollop of peach ice cream. But I really prefer a simpler dish, designed to feature the heart of palm.

WATERCRESS AND RADISH

Brought to America by the early settlers, watercress was raised in cool springs near homesteads. It got loose and now grows wild over much of the country. It can be picked from the wild, or it can be purchased fresh in most supermarkets. It is often used as a garnish or in salads—and is even used to make sandwiches.

For this salad, wash and dress the watercress, throwing out the larger stems. Shred some lettuce, mixing about half and half. Add some thinly sliced radishes, toss, and serve in salad bowls, with oil and vinegar bottles standing at the ready.

CRACKLINGS AND BACON BITS

Most people, guided perhaps by uninformed or misinformed cookbook authors (who ought to know better) and by supermarket fare, think that cracklings are made from pork skins. This is not the case. Pork skins are separate delicacies. The best cracklings are made from bits of fat, without the skin. I know a fellow near my place in

Wewahitchka, Florida, who drives to Colquit, Georgia, home of the annual mayhaw festival, to purchase skinless cracklings. My next-door neighbor goes a step farther, cooking off a large batch of skinless cracklings every month or so in his backyard. Healthy? This fellow has been making cracklings all his adult life, and he is now going on 86. Sometimes he eats the cracklings out of hand, and he often sprinkles a few on salads and baked potatoes.

Although most connoisseurs expect their cracklings to be made from pork fat, I sometimes use beef fat, usually trimmed from the steaks to be cooked. I also use duck fat from the breast, including (in this case) the skin. Of course, bacon without too much lean can be used to make excellent cracklings, which are sometimes called bacon bits.

In any case, dice the meat into sections no thicker or wider than ½ inch. Fry these in a cast-iron pot until they are brown and crisp. Drain well on absorbent paper. Serve as needed on salad, or sprinkle some on baked potatoes, possibly atop a dollop of sour cream.

Vegetables and Fruit

Steak and baked potatoes and good company occasion something nice for a side dish, such as steamed fiddleheads served only with melted butter and a little lemon juice. Wild-food enthusiasts may want to serve, in moderation, tips of catbrier or heart of cattail (sometimes called Cossack asparagus), if the guests be adventure-some. If the guests be culinary sports, try roasted Jerusalem artichokes or baked plantains instead of the usual baked potatoes. Or perhaps serve a cooked fruit instead of a vegetable, or maybe something com-pletely unexpected, such as a rutabaga puree or a chestnut puree, which is especially good with venison and wild boar steaks.

If you are grilling the steaks over charcoal, it's always nice to cook the vegetables and fruits along with the steaks. Grilled eggplant and grilled green tomato slices, for example.

In any case, here are some suggestions, along with my take on baking and serving a better potato.

BAKED POTATOES

Never wrap a potato in aluminum foil before baking. If you do, it will be partly steamed and will have a somewhat mushy texture. (If that's what you want, fine. But please peel off the foil before putting the potato on the table or plates.) Baking it without the foil will be more likely to give a flaky texture and a tougher skin. Of course, having the right baking potato—russet or Idaho—will help.

To proceed, select large, nicely shaped potatoes. Wash or (if you must) scrub them. Dry the potatoes and preheat the oven to 425 degrees. Grease the potatoes lightly with butter or olive oil. Bake in the center of the oven for about 25 minutes. Pull out the rack and puncture the skins on top with the tines of a fork; this will allow some steam to escape, giving you a more fluffy potato. Bake for another 20 minutes or longer, until done. (I usually squeeze mine quickly between thumb and forefinger. If they give, they are done.)

Serve hot, topped with butter, sour cream, chopped chives, or other toppings. I prefer sour cream sprinkled with freshly made cracklings. To fluff the potato for serving, prick the top with the tines of a fork, working about 80 percent of the length and breadth of the potato. Then, using the fingers of both hands, push the ends inward, causing the potato to burst in the middle, somewhat like a flower opening inside out. Sprinkle with salt and add the toppings. It's best to fluff the potatoes for your guests, in case they don't know the trick.

If you are short of time, you can "bake" an acceptable potato in a microwave oven. Grease the potato with a little peanut oil, puncture a few holes in it with a fork, wrap it loosely in a paper towel (which will allow the steam to escape), and cook on high in the center of the microwave for 5 or 6 minutes. The exact time will depend on your microwave and on the size of the potatoes. It's best to cook one potato at a time, centering it perfectly in the microwave. If you bunch several potatoes in the microwave, you may have hard spots here and there.

MASHED POTATOES

Modern cookbooks and magazine articles may be straining too hard to put a new spin on age-old recipes. Finding an uncluttered recipe even for mashed potatoes is no cinch these days. A recently revised cooking bible, said to have a sold in the millions, calls for butter, salt, white pepper, milk (or half-and-half or buttermilk), garlic, onion, celery (with leaves), and a bay leaf, along with the potatoes! Here's an older recipe, which I like to serve with hamburger steaks with gravy and baked dishes such as Swiss steak.

2 cups diced raw potatoes (peeled)	**2 tablespoons melted butter**
1 cup hot cream	**salt and pepper**

Boil the potatoes in a little salted water until tender. Drain. In a suitable bowl, mash the potatoes with a potato masher until smooth and fluffy. Add the butter and cream, along a little salt and pepper, blending well. Set the bowl over hot water until ready to serve, but do not overheat.

Note: Increase the measures as needed, allowing at least ½ cup of raw potatoes per person—I'll take more if you've got a good gravy to serve. Of course, these potatoes can also be served with a dollop of green peas in the center instead of or in addition to the gravy.

BOILED NEW POTATOES

New potatoes are simply immature potatoes, often a red variety, harvested before they are fully grown. Ideally, they should be no larger than a golf ball and fresh from the garden. The best ones, as I remember from my boyhood, are dug from around the growing plant with a large kitchen spoon, robbing one or two from each plant without overly stressing it. Red-skinned supermarket potatoes will do, but they tend to be a little too large and too long out of the ground. In either case, it's best to wash the potato—scrub it if you must—but do not peel it, and forget about the little eyes.

To proceed, heat a pot of lightly salted water (about 1 teaspoon per quart) to a boil. Add the potatoes, bring to a new boil, reduce the heat, cover, and simmer for 10 minutes or longer, until the potatoes are tender but not mushy. (The texture of new potatoes is part of the gustatory experience.) Drain off the hot water, but keep the potatoes in the pot, covered with a clean cloth, until time to serve. Serve hot with a little salt and pepper. Butter and sauces can be served, with the tops perhaps sprinkled with chopped fresh parsley—but really fresh new potatoes need no seasoning or garnish.

Note: New potatoes can also be steamed over a little water. Usually, steaming will take longer—but not much. In any case, do not overcook new potatoes.

ASPARAGUS

Asparagus spears make an ideal vegetable for serving with whole steaks, partly because of their flavor and partly because the spears stack so neatly around the meat. There are all manner of recipes for asparagus, many calling for sauces and various ingredients. In my book, however, simply steamed or boiled spears go best with steaks, using only a little salt and perhaps some melted butter.

A good deal depends on having good, fresh, tender spears. Often the smaller or younger, usually tender spears can be used from tip to butt. Older spears should be snapped off, using the tip end. The tough ends can be made more palpable by trimming off the fibrous outer coating with a vegetable peeler. Although asparagus can be broiled, grilled, or baked, I think it is best to stick with steamed or boiled whole spears. In a pinch, whole canned spears can be used, and are in my opinion better than old "fresh" spears. At its very best, asparagus should be cooked the same day it is gathered from the garden. Happy be the cook who has his own patch, or who knows a secret wild stand to stalk.

To steam asparagus, stand the spears upright in a tall steamer (some are made especially for asparagus). Place the steamer over 1 inch of boiling water, cover, and steam for about 6 minutes for medium-thick spears; 4 minutes for thin; or 9 to 10 minutes for thick. When done, the spears should be tender but slightly crisp—and bright green (unless you are using purple or cream asparagus, which isn't recommended here because the color green adds to the menu).

Of course, asparagus can also be steamed in a wide pan, laying the spears flat on a rack instead of upright.

To boil asparagus, place the spears flat in boiling water. I use about 10 cups of water with 1 tablespoon of salt. Cover and cook for about the same time as for steaming. When done, carefully remove and drain the spears, placing them flat on absorbent paper or on a serving platter.

FRENCH BEANS

If you don't have good fresh asparagus at hand, consider serving French-cut green beans. Snap off the ends of the beans and remove the string along the seam. Cut lengthwise into thin strips. Cook in a little salted boiling water until the beans are tender but not too soft. Drain the beans well and serve topped with a little melted butter.

ONION RINGS

Onion rings, properly fried, are good with most anything, and go especially well with gravy-producing steak recipes. I like them with steak burgers. It's best to use large, mild white onions, such as Vidalia. Peel off the outer layer, slice the onion into ⅜- to ½-inch wheels, and separate into rings. I also fry the centers, or serve them separately, raw, or in a salad.

onion rings	1 tablespoon salt
1 cup all-purpose flour	1 teaspoon baking powder
1 cup milk	peanut oil (or other good
1 chicken egg	cooking oil)

In a large batter bowl, mix the flour, baking powder, and salt. Mix in the milk and egg. Let the batter rest for 30 minutes. Rig for deep-frying, heating 3 or 4 inches of peanut oil, or more, to 375 degrees. Mix some of the onion rings in with the batter, drain each ring over the bowl, and place into the hot oil. Do not overcrowd. When the rings are browned, drain them over the deep-fryer, then drain them on a brown bag or other absorbent paper.

SKEWERED BUTTON MUSHROOMS

Some of the larger mushrooms, such as portabello, are easy to grill or broil right alongside the steaks. The smaller button mushrooms, however, work best when skewered. It's best to remove the stems, saving them for sauces and recipes calling for minced mushrooms. I like to cook these on small bamboo skewers, serving one for each person, right atop the steaks. These go nicely with any steak, but they are especially nice with grilled or broiled steaks. I allow about 4 ounces of button mushrooms per person.

button mushrooms   **salt**
melted butter   **lemon wedges**

Rig for grilling or broiling, presumably along with the steaks. Stem and wash the mushrooms. Put them into boiling water for 1 minute. Remove and dry with paper towels. Thread the mushrooms from side to side (leaving the tops and bottoms up and down) onto the skewers. Brush with melted butter, and sprinkle with salt. Grill over hot coals as the steaks cook, or for about 8 minutes, turning several times. Squeeze a drop or two of lemon juice on the stem end of each mushroom and serve warm either on the skewers or off.

SAUTÉED MUSHROOMS

One of my sons loves mushrooms, and he often brings home an 8-ounce package of button mushrooms for me to cook for him. He'll eat the whole works, but usually an 8-ounce package will feed two or more. If the mushrooms are small, I leave them whole, merely trimming off the end of the stem, which I also sauté and serve. If they are large, I usually slice them ¼ inch thick.

8 ounces fresh mushrooms   **3 tablespoons warm brandy**
3 tablespoons clarified   **salt and freshly ground**
    butter (chapter 12)   **black pepper**

In a large skillet, sauté the mushrooms in the butter until they are lightly browned. Pour in the brandy. Flame, shaking the skillet with one hand. Sprinkle with a little salt and pepper to taste. Serve hot with steak or with a thick, juicy hamburger steak.

GRILLED PINEAPPLE

Rig for grilling over hot coals, gas, or electric heat. Twist the top leaves off a fresh pineapple, cut it in half, and then cut each half in half. Slice off the core part. Grill the quarters about 4 inches from the heat for 20 minutes or so, turning often. When you are ready to serve, cut the pineapple quarters along the rind, freeing the fruit but leaving it sitting in the rind. Then cut the fruit into bite-size segments and serve in the rind as a side dish. This is especially good with grilled turkey steaks or pork. I'll also take some with a ribeye of beef. And with emu, too.

GRILLED BANANAS

Although bananas are often used in dessert dishes, they can also be served along with the meat course. It would, for example, be appropriate to serve grilled bananas with grilled pork steaks. Peel and cut each banana in half lengthwise. Heat a little honey in a skillet and toss the bananas in it to lightly coat all sides. Place the bananas flat-side down on the grill, about 4 inches above hot coals. Cook until the bottom is charred along the grid marks. Turn carefully and cook the other side. Using a spatula, place the slices on a serving platter and sprinkle lightly with freshly ground allspice and perhaps a little Hungarian paprika for color.

Note: When serving these bananas as a dessert, try serving two hot banana halves topped with a dollop or two of vanilla ice cream. See also bananas Foster later in this chapter.

BAKED PLANTAINS

These tropical vegetables—they contain more starch than bananas and must be cooked, usually baked or fried—are becoming more widely available these days in large supermarkets all across America. For this recipe, use fully ripe plantains, which will have blackened skins. I allow one plantain per person, proceeding as follows. Preheat the oven to 375 degrees. Cut off the ends of the plantains, then slit the skin lengthwise with a knife, but do not peel it back. Place the plantains on a rack, slit-side up, in the center of the oven. Bake for 40 minutes. Let cool a little. Peel back the skin from one end to the other. Drizzle with a little melted butter and fresh lime juice, squeezed to taste from lime quarters. Serve hot as a vegetable along with the steaks.

Note: There are other recipes for cooked plantains, either as a dessert or as a vegetable, and fried plantain chips are very tasty. A good deal depends on the ripeness of the plantain. For baking, the plantains should be quite black. (Don't worry; plantains hold their texture much better than bananas.) If properly baked when fully ripe, the plantain will be tender but not mushy and only slightly sweet.

Bread

For grilled or broiled steak, as well as for most skillet steaks, a crusty French or Italian bread will do the trick. Most people buy these in bakeries or from local grocery stores, and will have regional favorites. In addition to the large loaves, I like to serve French rolls from time to time. Be warned, however, that true French bread has a chewy crust and may not be for everybody. I like it hot with some melted butter.

For hamburger steaks and country steaks with plenty of gravy, try thick buttermilk biscuits instead of a loaf.

GARLIC BREAD

Use a loaf of French-type or sourdough bread. Make some diagonal cuts along the top, marking the servings, but do not cut all the way through. Heat ½ cup of butter in a saucepan and add 2 cloves crushed garlic. Heat for several minutes, allowing the flavors to mix. Brush the top of the loaf with the garlic butter. Then wrap it in heavy aluminum foil and heat it in a hot oven or on a grill, well away from the main heat. Serve the bread hot with plenty of fresh butter on the side for those who want it.

Desserts and After-Dinner Drinks

The best dessert is whatever you like, but I think a rather light offering, followed by a drink or two, is proper for finishing off a steak feast. Fresh fruit topped with real whipped cream is hard to beat.

ICE CREAM

Plain vanilla ice cream, perhaps topped with just a touch of colorful homemade pomegranate syrup, sloe gin, or some such colorful syrup of the world, or a little very good liqueur, always makes a nice dessert to finish off a steak meal. It is especially fitting in hot weather. A small piece of plain pound cake also goes nicely with ice cream if you are serving hot coffee on the side.

BANANAS FOSTER

This dish was invented some years ago at Brennan's restaurant in New Orleans and was billed, I understand, as breakfast fare. Not for me. I almost died (or so I thought at the time) from drinking too much banana rum during an all-night romp in Cuba many years ago, during my navy days. Ever since, I have been reluctant to combine rum and bananas during the morning hours. Brennan's bananas Foster, however, is so good that I like it as dessert after a big T-bone. For show, the dish is better if it is cooked at the table in a chafing dish. Some recipes call for rum and banana liqueur, but I can't go quite that far. I use cognac, in case I want to sip a little more, along with some strong coffee, after eating.

2 ripe bananas	lemon juice
¼ cup butter	cinnamon, ground
⅓ cup brown sugar	nutmeg, freshly grated
¼ cup dark rum	very good vanilla ice cream
1 tablespoon cognac	

Cut the bananas in half lengthwise, then divide each piece in fourths crosswise. Baste the pieces with lemon juice. In a blazer pan, heat the butter and sugar, stirring constantly, until the sugar melts. Add the banana pieces, flat-side down, and cook for 2 minutes. Turn each banana piece and cook for another 2 minutes. Turn off the heat. Sprinkle the bananas lightly with ground cinnamon and a little grated nutmeg. Heat the rum and cognac in a saucepan, ignite the mixture with a match, and pour it flaming over the bananas. Immediately serve the bananas over a bed of rich vanilla ice cream.

Note: The measures in this recipe will do for four people who have eaten a T-bone each. If you have served your guests only a little dab of tenderloin, double the measures for bananas Foster.

WHIPPED CREAM

The cream to whip is sold these days in small containers, but I can remember my mother and my aunts skimming it off the top of unpasteurized milk from the family cow. We sometimes called it top milk. Anyhow, be sure you use "heavy cream" or "whipping cream." It's best to use cream with a butterfat content of at least 30 to 40 percent; the higher the better for whipping. If you are whipping the cream by hand, use a balloon-type whisk and give it a sort of upward roll. The idea is to incorporate as much air as possible. This process can be speeded up by whipping the cream in a bowl suspended over a larger bowl of ice. If you overwork the cream, however, it may be too buttery, in which case you may have to start over. So, be careful with electric beaters. I've got a small battery-operated hand mixer that works fine.

I normally use a little vanilla and confectioner's sugar in any whipped cream to be used in desserts, and I have included these ingredients in the list below. These measures yield about 2 cups of whipped cream.

1 cup heavy whipping cream, cold

1 tablespoon confectioner's sugar (optional)

1 tablespoon vanilla (optional)

Whip the cream in a cool bowl until it starts to stiffen. Slowly add the sugar and vanilla, whipping as you go. Continue to whip until soft peaks form and the volume doubles, or thereabouts. Use the whipped cream right away. It can be stored in the refrigerator for an hour or so, but a liquid may begin to accumulate in the bottom of the bowl.

GREEN MANGO FOOL

This old British recipe calls for green mangos. These should be firm and hard—which is the state of most of the mangos in my local supermarkets, at least during their first few days on the shelf. This dish is best when served with a small slice of plain pound cake, which can be made at home or purchased at the bakery.

2 green mangos	**1 recipe whipped cream**
⅓ cup sugar	**(see recipe above)**
⅓ cup water	**pound cake (precooked)**

Peel the mangos and cut the flesh away from the pit as best you can. Then dice the flesh and place it into a saucepan, along with the sugar and water. Cook for about 10 minutes, stirring as you go, until the mango is soft. Add a little more sugar if the mango tastes too tart, bearing in mind that the whipped cream will also be sweet. Mash the mango with a fork until it is the consistency of applesauce. Chill the mango while you prepare the whipped cream. Then gently fold the mango puree into the cream, leaving streaks of mango in the white cream. Serve the mango fool in stemmed dessert dishes or low stemmed glasses with a small slice of pound cake on the side.

Note: You can also use this recipe with ripe mangos if you can't find green ones. Simply peel and puree the mangos without cooking them. Then add a little sugar to taste along with the juice of 1 large lemon or lime. Stir and chill. Then fold into the whipped cream. Also, try 4 kiwi fruits instead of the ripe mangos, adding sugar to taste and the juice of 1 large lemon or lime. If you have suitable fresh fruit in your garden, such as blueberries or loquats, mash these and substitute for the mango, with or without lemon juice, to taste.

IRISH COFFEE

I consider this one to be the ultimate after-dinner drink, and it can also double as a dessert. But limit it to one. If you want to do some serious after-dinner drinking, try brandy or perhaps Scotch and water. Be warned that the coffee must be hot and strong, whereas some coffeemakers produce only a warm brew and some brewers confuse coffee with tea. The measures below will make one drink, and, of course, each drink is made separately. It's a nice touch to grind the coffee grounds and brew the coffee while the guests wait. Fresh coffee is always best, and smells good.

hot black coffee, freshly brewed
1 jigger Irish whiskey (exactly
   1½ ounces)

1 teaspoon brown sugar
whipped cream (sweetened,
   as in the recipe above)

When the coffee is ready, warm two Irish coffee glasses or suitable goblets by rinsing them in very hot water. Pour the coffee and Irish whiskey into the glass. Add the sugar, stirring until it has dissolved. Top with a dollop of whipped cream, but do not stir. Serve immediately.

Saucing the Steak

12

I'M NOT MUCH for sousing a good medium-rare steak, full of its own flavor and juices, with thick sauces. I don't even want some of this stuff on my table, but, as a host and as a writer, I must honor the habits of others. Still, I'll leave the A-1 in the refrigerator until somebody requests it. On the other hand, a good sauce can add interest and flavor to some dishes, and some are especially good with venison and boar. If, as expected, our beef will gradually become less and less marbled with juicy fat, sauces may play a more important role in my suggested menu. Today I find that a sauce goes best with a lean cut, such as flank steak. But, of course, pan sauces are a necessary part of some classic skillet recipes. Some of these are set forth in the chapter on skillet cookery. Here are a few more:

Deglazing the Pan
The very best steak sauces are made with the pan drippings resulting from cooking steak in a skillet or broiling pan. When making most of these, the cook will "deglaze the pan," usually by adding wine or some such liquid and scraping any dredgings from the bottom, which will become part of the sauce. It's best, always, to scrape and stir with a wooden spatula or wooden spoon.

EASY PAN SAUCE

Although it's usually easy to make a sauce from pan drippings when you cook a steak or chop in a skillet or in a pan under a broiler, what you put into the mix might depend on what you have cooked, how it was marinated, and so on, so that the flavors don't clash. The measures below work for a medium-size skillet. If the meat doesn't yield 2 tablespoons of drippings, fill in with a little butter or cooking oil.

2 tablespoons pan drippings from the meat	**½ cup red wine**
	salt and black pepper

Over low heat, scrape up the pan dredgings with a spatula, mixing with the pan drippings. Add the red wine, salt, and pepper. Cook on high heat for a minute or two.

Variations: Instead of red wine, use beef broth or cream. If you want a thick brown gravy instead of sauce (if I may make the distinction), put 1 or 2 tablespoons of flour into the pan drippings along with salt and pepper. Heat and stir, as when making a roux, slowly mixing in enough hot broth or water to make a thick gravy. Personally, I want the thinner sauce on ribeyes and such served with a baked potato; the thicker gravy on burger steaks served with mashed potatoes or rice.

Other Homemade Sauces

Most cookbooks contain recipes for standard European sauces, such as sauce Colbert or châteaubriand sauce. These recipes may look simple enough, but don't proceed before you check all the ingredients very carefully; some sauces call for other several other sauces and will have you hopscotching about in the tome. If you don't watch out you may be in the kitchen for two days. I'm not joking. And you'll need a list of ingredients as long as your leg. A recipe in one book for what would on first thought seem be a simple brown sauce contains, in addition to a number of herbs and spices, the following: veal bones, beef bones, a chicken carcass, marrow fat, diced ham, and 1 cup of game stew meat.

Anyhow, there are entire books on sauces, and I bow to these in case anyone has the time. Meanwhile, several of the sauces below are better suited for venison and game steaks, because, frankly, these meats are leaner and need saucing more than a juicy well-marbled beefsteak.

GREAT NORTHERN STEAK SAUCE

Here's a sauce from the Great Northern Railway Company. It's easy to mix and comes in handy for serving a crowd. It can be refrigerated and reheated.

1 pound butter
¾ cup Worcestershire sauce
juice of 3 lemons
1 clove garlic, minced

6 teaspoons dry mustard
6 teaspoons sugar
salt and freshly ground
    black pepper

Melt the butter. Mix in the mustard and sugar, stirring as you go. Simmer—but do not boil. Stir in the rest of the ingredients. Serve hot.

CHURRASCO SAUCE

Here's an Argentine recipe that's good for saucing beef, venison, rhea, and other good red meats. I sometimes make it with wild onions.

2 cups minced green onions
    with about half the tops
1 cup white wine
½ cup white wine vinegar
½ pound butter

1 tablespoon freshly ground
    black pepper
salt
minced fresh rosemary
    (optional)

Cut off a lump of butter (about 1 tablespoon) and set it aside. Heat the rest of the butter in a skillet. Sauté the green onions for 5 or 6 minutes. Add the wine, wine vinegar, pepper, and salt, along with a little fresh rosemary. Bring to a boil, reduce the heat, and simmer for a few minutes. Add the lump of butter and swirl.

Note: A similar Argentinean creation, *chimichurri,* is made with parsley instead of green onions. Sometimes hot peppers or chili powder are added.

ALASKAN JUNIPER SAUCE

Juniper berries, used to flavor gin, are really little cones, not true berries. They are widely used in northern Europe as a spice, popular in cooking venison and other game and wild fowl. The berries can be picked from juniper trees in the wild and dried at home, or they can be purchased in some supermarkets and spice outlets. It's best to store (or buy) the berries whole, then crush them as needed with a mortar and pestle, or pound them between sheets of wax paper. The stock used in this recipe can be made from bouillon cubes if necessary.

1 cup beef or game stock	1 tablespoon crushed
½ cup red wine	dried juniper berries
2 tablespoons butter	salt and pepper
2 tablespoons flour	

Melt the butter on low heat and stir in the flour. Cook and stir, cook and stir, until the mixture turns light brown. Slowly add the stock and simmer for 10 minutes or so, stirring a time or two. Stir in the crushed juniper berries, wine, salt, and pepper. Simmer until the consistency of the sauce suits you. Thin the sauce if necessary with a little more stock. Serve with venison or wild fowl.

CAPE COD GAME SAUCE

Here's a delicious sauce made with the aid of stewed cranberries. It's best to use fresh or frozen cranberries, wild or commercial, which I usually keep in my freezer year-round. The broth used in the recipe can be from beef, chicken, or venison. I'll allow the use of bouillon cubes or granules dissolved in water.

2 cups broth

1 cup cranberries

3 tablespoons butter

2 tablespoons flour

½ teaspoon salt

Put the cranberries into a small saucepan, add a little water, and simmer for 10 minutes or so. In another saucepan, melt the butter and stir in the flour. Slowly pour in the stock. Add the salt and simmer over low heat until the mixture thickens, stirring as you go to smooth it out. Stir in the stewed cranberries. Simmer for 5 minutes. Serve warm or chilled.

GREEN PEPPERCORN SAUCE FOR FISH STEAKS

The green peppercorns used in this recipe, available in spice markets, should come packed in water.

8 ounces sour cream

2 tablespoon green peppercorns, crushed

crushed sea salt to taste

Mix all the ingredients in a serving bowl, cover, and refrigerate. Serve chilled, smeared sparingly over hot grilled or broiled fish steaks.

CURRANT SAUCE

Here's an old-time sauce, similar to maître d'hotel butter, that still goes nicely with hot venison steaks. It calls for red currant jelly, available commercially, but homemade jelly from any wild currant (as well as from mayhaws, buffaloberries, beach plums, or cranberries) can also be used.

1 cup butter	**2 teaspoons black pepper**
¼ cup red currant jelly	**½ teaspoon salt**
¼ cup chopped fresh parsley	

Melt the butter in a saucepan on low heat. Stir in the other ingredients and steep for 10 or 15 minutes. Use warm or at room temperature, but stir before serving.

MUSCADINE VENISON SAUCE

Here's a sauce that I make with the aid of wild muscadines (often called bullaces) or with scuppernoggs. Both are large grapes with a tough, tart skin. Thin-skinned grapes can also be used, but the sauce may lose some of its characteristic tart flavor.

1½ cups whole muscadines	**¼ cup mushrooms, minced**
½ cup red wine	**¼ cup butter**
½ cup pecans or hickory nuts, minced	**¼ teaspoon freshly ground allspice**

Put the grapes into a saucepan, almost cover with water, and bring to a boil. Cover, reduce the heat, and simmer for 10 minutes or so. Pop the pulp from the grapes and mince the tart skins. Press the pulp through a sieve to remove the seeds. Add the butter to the saucepan, along with the pulp and the minced skins. Stir in the wine, mushrooms, and allspice. Simmer for 5 or 6 minutes. Stir in the pecans, heat through, and serve hot over venison steaks.

WYOMING KETCHUP

This great sweet-and-sour recipe calls for the buffaloberries that grow wild on the northwestern plains and up into Canada. It can also be made with cranberries, fresh or frozen.

1 quart wild buffaloberry pulp	1½ tablespoons freshly crushed allspice berries
2⅔ cups sugar	1 teaspoon salt
1⅓ cups vinegar	⅛ teaspoon cayenne

Mix and simmer all the ingredients in a suitable saucepan, stirring as you go, until it thickens to suit you. Serve on venison, bear, or other wild game—and duck.

GREEN MINT SAUCE

Mint sauce, traditionally used with lamb and mutton, also goes nicely with venison, bighorn, and other game. I like to make it with peppermint or spearmint, both of which grow wild just about everywhere in North America.

1 cup fresh wild mint leaves	¼ cup apple cider vinegar
1½ cups water	green food coloring
1 cup sugar	(optional)

Wash the mint leaves in cool water and chop them. In a saucepan, mix the water, vinegar, and sugar; bring to a boil, reduce the heat, and simmer for 10 minutes. Remove the saucepan from the heat, stir in the chopped mint leaves, and steep for 1 hour. Strain the liquid into a serving jar and color with a drop or two of green food coloring.

MUSHROOM KETCHUP

This recipe takes some time to prepare, but the result can be refrigerated for use in cooking several steaks. The flavor, intense and full of salt, make it suitable for using in small amounts, like fish sauce or soy sauce, as an ingredient in other sauces or skillet sauces.

Often edible wild mushrooms are found in large batches, free for the picking. Whenever you run across a bonanza, you may want to try this old British recipe. Or you can purchase fresh mushrooms at the market. The ordinary button mushrooms work nicely. You'll need several pounds of mushrooms. Weigh them, break them up or slice them, then spread them out and sprinkle with 1 tablespoon of salt per pound of mushrooms. Next, layer the mushrooms in a crock large enough to hold them. (Never use a metal container.) Leave them to sweat out their juices for three days, pressing them from time to time to help things along. Next, put the crock into a slow oven— on the lowest setting—for 3 hours. (I sometimes combine the first two steps by using a standard Crock-Pot.) Then put the juice and mushrooms into a piece of nylon netting or cotton cloth over a suitable container. Squeeze out the juice, discarding the pulp. Measure the juice. Note that the recipe below is for 1 quart of juice; scale the measures up or down as required. As a rule of thumb, 3 pounds of mushrooms will yield 1 quart of juice, which in turn will reduce to 1 cup of sauce.

1 quart mushroom juice	**½ teaspoon grated nutmeg**
1 cup red wine	**½ teaspoon grated fresh**
4 cloves garlic, minced	**gingerroot**
red chili pepper (hot)	**cornstarch paste (optional)**

Put the mushroom juice and wine into a saucepan and heat. Tie the garlic, red chili pepper (pricked with a fork), ginger, and nutmeg in a cotton bag, then put it into the juice. Simmer uncovered for 2 or 3 hours, or until the liquid thickens a little and is reduced to only 25 percent of its original volume. At this point, the sauce will be on the thin side (as compared with commercial tomato ketchup). If you want it thicker, stir in a little cornstarch paste during the last few minutes of cooking. Place the liquid in sterilized jars and process in boiling water for 20 minutes. Serve warm or chilled.

In addition to topping cooked steaks, this mushroom sauce (preferably thin) is great as a last-minute basting sauce for grilled meats. Be sure to add a little to the gravy the next time you cook a big hamburger steak in your favorite skillet.

Note: A revised version of a classic American cookbook (the same one that tells us to wash steaks after cooking them in a salt-lined skillet) gives a similar recipe—but advises the reader to throw out the liquid, no doubt because it will be salty, and use what's left of the mushrooms. Don't do so if you want flavor.

Commercial Sauces

A lot of people want some kind of sauce on the table when steak is served up for dinner. Other kinds of sauces are used for basting the steak during cooking, and sometimes for marinating the steak for a few minutes prior to cooking. (This topic overlaps somewhat with the marinade heading, and some of the sauces are covered briefly in both categories.)

A-1 STEAK SAUCE. This popular commercial sauce, widely available, is based on tomatoes, various citrus products, vinegar, and other ingredients. It is often used as a table condiment, usually served in the bottle at informal tables. Variations on the basic A-1 include Bold & Spicy, Bold & Spicy with Tabasco, Thick & Hearty, Sweet & Tangy.

DALE'S STEAK SEASONING. Popular in some parts of the country for half a century, this is a thin, concentrated sauce used mostly as a quick marinade or as an ingredient in a basting sauce. My oldest son likes a steak marinade made with half Dale's and half dry red wine, and, for basting thick pork T-bones, I like to mix 3 parts Dale's and 1 part red wine vinegar. I also use a baste made with half Dale's and half melted butter. Essentially, Dale's is heavy on soy sauce, along with onion, garlic, gingerroot, and spices.

LEA & PERRINS STEAK SAUCE. Some writers use "Lea & Perrins" to refer to Worcestershire sauce, the firm's mainstay for many years. They are, however, now marketing a steak sauce.

LONDON PUB. Billed as a steak and chop sauce, this import from England is widely available in American markets. It contains tomatoes, apple pulp, soy sauce, and various other ingredients and spices. Use it primarily as a rather spicy sauce (not a marinade or baste) for plainly grilled or broiled steaks or chops.

MYRON'S 20-GAUGE. A magical blend of naturally brewed soy sauce, red wine, olive oil, garlic, honey, and other ingredients and spices, 20-Gauge is recommended as a cooking and basting sauce for game, beefsteaks, and other meats. It's also good as a table sauce. I like it mixed half and half with butter as a last-minute baste for grilled or broiled steaks and portabello mushrooms. If I had to choose one sauce for cooking purposes, it would be Myron's 20-Gauge. Myron (Chef Myron Becker) also offers several other sauces for fish, poultry, and other meats.

OYSTER SAUCE. This excellent sauce is made primarily from oysters and salt, along with the natural juice. Thick like ketchup, it is used in cooking and as a table condiment. One brand or another is widely available these days in the Chinese section of American supermarkets. It's good stuff, if you like the flavor of oysters, and can be used in skillet sauces or perhaps as a baste during the last few minutes of grilling or broiling.

PICKAPEPPA SAUCE. This mildly hot, spicy sauce from Jamaica goes nicely on a steak, especially for those who like A-1 and similar products. It contains chili pepper, tamarind, onions, tomatoes, cane vinegar, and other ingredients, aged in oak barrels for a minimum of a year. It is widely available in supermarkets. Good stuff.

WORCESTERSHIRE SAUCE. Several versions of this colonial-era British sauce are available, and all contain Asian ingredients adapted from India. Soy sauce, anchovies (or perhaps fish sauce), and tamarind define Worcestershire sauce. Usually it is considered an ingredient in recipes, but sometimes it is served directly on steaks as a sauce or perhaps as a marinade. Use it sparingly, if you like the flavor of steak.

HOT PEPPER SAUCES. There are hundreds of hot pepper sauces on the market. The most famous is made from the Tabasco pepper. Some others, often billed as Louisiana hot sauce, are made from cayenne peppers. Still others, hotter now, are made from habañero or Scotch bonnet fireballs. Most of these are red sauces, but green ones made from jalapeños are becoming more readily available. Ingredients vary, but usually such a hot sauce contains vinegar, salt, and chili peppers, with the emphasis on the chili peppers. But many other ingredients, including sherry, are also used. Some sauces, such as Pickapeppa (above) and Dat'l-Do-It (made with dayctal peppers that are grown in Florida), contain so much other stuff that I consider them to be "sauce" but not "pepper sauce."

Most of the true pepper sauces are too hot for use straight. I will allow a drop on an oyster or a drop or two on canned sardines, but not on a steak. They go nicely, however, as an ingredient in sauces and marinade.

SOY SAUCE. Invented in China, this fermented brew is made from soybeans, brine, and a grain such as wheat. Like wine, it takes time to bring out the true flavor. There are dozens of kinds and perhaps hundreds of brands, usually variations on basic light and dark sauces. As a general rule, dark sauce, like red wine, goes better with red meat and compound sauces destined for use with red meat. Japanese soy sauce, sometimes called *shoyu* sauce, typically contains more wheat and less soybean; it is less salty and is "lighter" than the Chinese sauces. Other Asian countries, such as Korea, have their own take on soy sauces.

In any case, any of the soy sauces available in American markets can be used directly on steaks (sparingly) or used as an ingredient in other sauces. It is the base for many commercial sauces and sops such as Dale's Steak Seasoning. If you use soy sauce by itself, consider it a seasoning. As a marinade, use it very sparingly on steaks—and apply it about 20 minutes before cooking.

FISH SAUCE. Fish sauce goes back to the ancient Romans, who called it *garnum*. In modern times, the people of Southeast Asia also use fish sauce in recipes and as a table condiment. Called *nuoc mam* in Vietnam, *nam pla* in Thailand, *tuk tey* in Cambodia, and *patis* in the Philippines, it is made by salting down anchovies or other small fish and catching the highly nutritious drippings. Several brands of fish sauce are now available in American markets. The stuff has a long shelf life and does not require refrigeration.

Use a little fish sauce as an ingredient in your steak sauces, or sprinkle some over salads and other foods. But use it sparingly; it is very salty and has a strong flavor.

SALSA AND BARBECUE SAUCES. In recent years, thousands of salsa recipes have been devised by cookbook and magazine writers, TV and restaurant chefs, and home cooks. Quite a few are available commercially, and in our supermarkets these sauces now outsell even tomato ketchup. Most of the widely available commercial salsas, sometimes billed as taco sauce or picante sauce, are based on tomatoes. All of these are good and can be used to top a steak, or they can be added to the pan juices to make a hot sauce. Personally, I don't care too much for tomato-based sauces (or tomato-based barbecue sauce) on steaks during the cooking process, but I don't rule them out. Also, we are seeing more and more "salsas" based on the green husk tomatoes and on various tropical fruits. A good mango-based salsa, for example, goes nicely with a hotly spiced blackened steak.

Barbecue sauces, usually based on tomatoes, are also available by the thousands. In general, I don't think these go too well with steaks, although I know I'll get some arguments on this. Barbecue sauces are at their best for slow-cooking pork ribs and other cuts of pork. If they are used on grilled steaks, apply them only during the last few minutes of cooking, especially if they contain sugar as well as tomatoes.

I won't go so far as to say that people who put ketchup on good steaks are not welcome at my table, but I really would prefer to serve them up a large hamburger steak instead of T-bone.

Steak Butters

Fresh butter makes a good cooking aid, or last-minute baste, for cooking steaks, and pats of butter, plain or seasoned, often top a sizzling-hot steak just before serving. Here are some comments and suggestions.

MAÎTRE D'HOTEL BUTTER

I make this classic butter often with the aid of a small battery-powered mixer that stands at ready on my countertop. Larger blenders can also be used.

1 cup softened butter, salted	¼ cup minced chives
¼ cup minced fresh parsley	¼ cup freshly squeezed lemon juice

Blend the butter, parsley, and chives with a blender or electric mixer. Slowly add the lemon juice, mixing as you go. Spread out some wax paper. Turn the butter mixture onto the wax paper, shape into a log, and roll it in the paper. Chill in the refrigerator or freezer. Cut into pats for serving with steaks or chops.

Note: This butter can also be melted and brushed onto the steak during the last minutes of broiling or grilling.

ANCHOVY STEAK BUTTER

Salty canned anchovies are used in various kinds of sauces, and the flavor, used in moderation, goes nicely with beef. Here's an easy way to serve it, allowing your guests the option of using it or not. Anchovy paste is available (packaged like toothpaste) in most supermarkets these days. A little goes a long way.

1 cup butter
½ cup finely chopped
   fresh parsley
¼ cup Worcestershire
   sauce
1 teaspoon anchovy paste

¼ teaspoon Hungarian
   paprika
⅛ teaspoon garlic powder
⅛ teaspoon freshly ground
   black pepper

In a blender, mix the butter, Worcestershire sauce, and anchovy paste. Add the parsley, paprika, garlic powder, and black pepper. Blend well. Shape the mixture into logs about 1 inch in diameter. Wrap each log in foil and freeze until needed. Cut the log into slices about ¼ inch thick and serve atop cooked steaks. This butter can also be used to make a pan gravy after cooking steaks in a skillet.

HERB BUTTER

This butter goes nicely on steaks of all kinds. Use fresh herbs if available, or use dried herbs in half measures. The ingredients lists calls for tarragon, but other herbs and mixes can be used to taste.

¼ pound butter, softened
1 tablespoon finely
   chopped tarragon

juice of 1 medium lemon
salt and freshly ground
   black pepper

Place the butter in a bowl, mashing it with the back of a spoon. Add the rest of the ingredients, a little at a time, and mix thoroughly. Shape the mixture into a roll about 1½ inches in diameter. Roll in wax paper and refrigerate. Slice for serving, topping each steak with a pat or two.

RUM BUTTER

This versatile butter is best used on grilled, broiled, or skillet steaks, preferably rather plain and unmarinated. See the Jamaican steak recipe in chapter 3.

½ cup unsalted butter
⅓ cup Jamaican rum,
    preferably golden
juice of 1 medium lime

2 tablespoons minced fresh cilantro
    or parsley
2 tablespoons minced shallots
salt and freshly ground black pepper

In a saucepan, simmer together the rum, shallots, salt, and black pepper, reducing the mix by half. Add the lime juice, parsley, and butter, stirring well. Pour the mixture into a butter mold, or other small mold, and refrigerate. (Or roll it in wax paper.) Slice into patties and serve atop cooked hot beefsteaks or pork chops as needed.

CLARIFIED BUTTER OR GHEE

Plain butter contains solids that burn or brown easily, causing problems when cooking over high heat. When the solids are removed, the butter works better, without burning, at higher temperature. It is called clarified butter or ghee, a term from Indian cookery.

Heat the butter slowly in a saucepan and skim off the scum that rises to the top. Then remove the butter from the heat and let it sit, allowing another set of impurities to settle to the bottom. Then pour the clarified butter off, leaving the sediment. Use this in any recipe that calls for cooking with butter on high heat, as in certain skillet steaks.

Marinades and Dry Rubs

There are three reasons for marinating steaks in a liquid. The first is to alter the flavor of the meat with spices and herbs and such ingredients as lemon juice or vinegar or Worcestershire sauce. The second is to get rid of a perceived strong flavor, as in venison. The third is to help tenderize the meat.

Because I like the flavor of beef and feel that most of the better steak cuts really don't require tenderization, I don't put too much stock in marinades, although I use them from time to time, sometimes when testing out somebody else's recipe. But there are other opinions, and sometimes a marinade is a important part of a recipe. In such cases, I include the marinade and its ingredients as part of the recipes in the various chapters.

Here are a few other marinades that may come in handy from time to time. But I'll have to be honest here: They really won't save the day with bad beef or game that has not been handled properly. Nothing can, and the wise cook, not wanting to be held responsible, will refuse such meats to start with.

To tenderize steak, the marinade must contain either an acidic ingredient (such as lemon juice, wine, or vinegar) or the juices of such natural tenderizers as papaya or kiwi.

MILK

Ordinary cow's milk makes a very good marinade for red meats. Simply cover the meat with milk in a nonmetallic container and marinate in the refrigerator overnight. Buttermilk also makes a good marinade, and I especially like it for tougher steaks destined to be beaten with a meat mallet, dusted with flour, and cooked in a skillet with a little oil. The buttermilk gravy, if properly made, is sometimes better than the steak, served over steaming hot jumbo biscuit halves.

BAKING SODA

One of my favorite marinades for venison steaks, or other game and ducks, calls for 1 tablespoon baking soda to 1 quart of water. In this simple solution I soak the meat overnight in the refrigerator, using a nonmetallic container. The solution helps the meat come out fresh, clean looking, and sweet smelling.

OLIVE OIL

I have used several kinds of oil as a marinade, including bacon drippings. But olive oil is my favorite, especially if I can get some that has some flavor of the olive. More often than not, I use some other ingredient along with the olive oil, such as cracked black pepper or crushed garlic. In any case, I simply brush the oil heavily on the steaks and set them aside for 30 minutes or longer at room temperature. Usually I stack the steaks.

JAMES BEARD'S TENDERIZING MARINADE

The great American Grillmaster billed this as one of his favorite marinades, used for soaking tough pieces of meat before the cookout. I find that it works nicely on chuck steaks and flank steaks to be broiled or grilled.

½ cup olive oil	3 tablespoons chopped
½ cup bourbon	fresh ginger
½ cup soy sauce	1 teaspoon dry mustard
2 small to medium onions,	1 teaspoon freshly ground
thinly sliced	black pepper
2 cloves garlic, chopped	1 teaspoon wine vinegar

Mix all the ingredients and use for marinating the meat for 6 to 24 hours. Also use it as a basting sauce. I prefer to throw out the old marinade and use fresh sauce as a baste.

LEMON MARINADE

This marinade works best on the less tender cuts of beef that are destined for the broiler or grill.

1 cup olive oil	**1 clove garlic, crushed**
juice of 1 lemon	**salt and freshly ground black pepper**

Mix all the ingredients and pour over the steak in a nonmetallic container. Marinate overnight in the refrigerator.

CALIFORNIA MARINADE

Here's a mix that works as a marinade on steaks destined for the grill or broiler. It can also be used as a basting sauce.

1 cup good red California wine	**3 springs fresh rosemary**
	3 sprigs fresh thyme
1 cup olive oil	**3 sprigs fresh marjoram**
3 cloves garlic, crushed	**1 bay leaf**

Mix all the ingredients and refrigerate for a day or so. Strain the mixture and use the liquid to marinate the steaks. To proceed, cover the meat in a nonmetallic container and place it in the refrigerator from 6 to 24 hours.

Soy Sauce, Teriyaki, Etc.

Soy sauce and various Asian sauces, including some steak "seasonings," work marinade-wonders if used sparingly and for a relatively short period of time. Usually 30 minutes will do the trick.

Small measures of such sauces, including Worcestershire, can, of course, be used with other liquids to formulate marinades for longer soaking. A basic recipe would call for equal parts of soy sauce, rice wine or sherry, and oil, along with maybe garlic or fresh gingerroot.

See also the entries under the heading Commercial Sauces, above.

DRY RUBS

Some cooks like to rub various dry ingredients into the surface of a steak and let it rest for 30 minutes or so before cooking. Usually, the idea is to alter the flavor of the meat. In addition to private recipes, a number of such rubs are being marketed, including Jamaica jerk rub and various Cajun dusts and ground spices.

For my personal use, I can do without all this stuff except for one basic dry ingredient: black pepper. Freshly cracked or coarsely ground black pepper, pressed into the meat, can impart a wonderful flavor to steaks and is used in such classic recipes as steak au poivre.

I seldom use salt (or the various seasoning salts) to rub a steak or any other meat until I get ready to cook, or, better, long after the cooking has started. Some purists insist that the salt be held for use at the table. In any case, salting the meat too early draws out the moisture, which is why it is used so widely in curing and jerking meats and fish.

Cooking Aids and Ingredients

Here are a few topics that should be addressed before we leave this book, hopefully to cook up a steak or two.

LIQUID SMOKE. This product works and is widely available in supermarkets. Use as directed in individual recipes, or use sparingly in any baste. Personally, I prefer the real thing to Liquid Smoke, and, in general, smoke isn't as important in steak cookery as it is in cooking pork ribs and chicken and other barbecue treats.

MEAT TENDERIZERS. There are several commercial shake-on meat tenderizers on the market. Most steaks don't need these, but some do.

It's best to follow the directions on the product's box or package. Natural tenderizers include papaya fruit and kiwi fruits, and marinades with acidic ingredients.

HERBS. Some recipes call for herbs of one sort or another. It's always best to use fresh herbs, if available. I like to raise my own, and I try to freeze some for year-round use. Dried herbs will do in most cases in which garnish is not important. If the recipe calls for fresh herbs, reduce the amount by half if you use dried, as a rule of thumb.

BLACK PEPPER. This is the one spice that I would really miss in steak cookery. It's almost always best to buy whole peppercorns and grind them as needed. Freshly ground pepper has more flavor and a wonderful aroma. I use preground pepper from time to time, and I confess to sometimes using coarsely ground black pepper in steak au poivre to save a little time. Always, put a pepper mill on the table for people who want some freshly ground pepper on their salad or a little more on their steak.

SALT. Any table salt will do but I prefer sea salt, which is becoming more widely available these days. You can buy it in several grades and by size. For table use, I like a coarse salt and a salt mill, similar to a pepper mill. I always salt my food to taste, and I don't want to eat without it. Salt is an essential ingredient for a good meal.

Index